Thinking
Theologically

Elements of Preaching

O. Wesley Allen Jr., series editor

Thinking Theologically
The Preacher as Theologian
Ronald J. Allen

Knowing the Context
Frames, Tools, and Signs for Preaching
James R. Nieman

Interpreting the Bible
Exegetical Approaches for Preaching
Mary Foskett

Shaping the Claim
Moving from Text to Sermon
Marvin McMickle

Determining the Form
Structures for Preaching
O. Wesley Allen Jr.

Finding Language and Imagery
The Custody of Holy Speech
Jennifer L. Lord

Delivering the Sermon
Voice, Body, and Animation in Proclamation
Teresa L. Fry Brown

Serving the Word
Preaching in Worship
Melinda A. Quivik

Thinking Theologically

The Preacher as Theologian

Ronald J. Allen

Fortress Press
Minneapolis

To
John W. McKiernan
for helping give birth to Linda
and
Mercedes Altizer McKiernan
for helping give rebirth to John

THINKING THEOLOGICALLY
The Preacher as Theologian

Copyright © 2008 Fortress Press, an imprint of Augsburg Fortress. All rights reserved. Except for brief quotations in critical articles or reviews, no part of this book may be reproduced in any manner without prior written permission from the publisher. Visit http://www.augsburg-fortress.org/copyrights/contact.asp or write to Permissions, Augsburg Fortress, Box 1209, Minneapolis, MN 55440.

Scripture passages are from the New Revised Standard Version of the Bible, copyright © 1989 National Council of the Churches of Christ in the USA. Used by permission. All rights reserved.

Cover image: © iStockphoto.com/Igor Skrynnikov
Cover and book design: John Goodman

Library of Congress Cataloging-in-Publication Data
Allen, Ronald J. (Ronald James), 1949-
Thinking theologically : the preacher as theologian / Ronald J. Allen.
    p. cm. — (Elements of preaching)
Includes bibliographical references.
ISBN 978-0-8006-6232-5 (alk. paper)
1. Theology—History—20th century. 2. Preaching. I. Title.
BT78.A45 2007
230'.046—dc22   2007035074

The paper used in this publication meets the minimum requirements of American National Standard for Information Sciences—Permanence of Paper for Printed Library Materials, ANSI Z329.48-1984.

Manufactured in the U.S.A.

12   11   10   09   08   1   2   3   4   5   6   7   8   9   10

Contents

Editor's Foreword

Preparing beginning preachers to stand before the body of Christ and proclaim the word of God faithfully, authentically, and effectively Sunday after Sunday is and always has been a daunting responsibility. As North American pastors face pews filled with citizens of a postmodern, post-Christendom culture, this teaching task becomes even more complex. The theological, exegetical, and homiletical skills that preachers need for the future are as much in flux today as they ever have been in Western Christianity. Thus providing seminary students with a solid but flexible homiletical foundation at the start of their careers is a necessity.

Traditionally, professors of preaching choose a primary introductory textbook that presents a theology of proclamation and a process of sermon development and delivery from a single point of view. To maintain such a singular point of view is the sign of good writing, but it does at times cause problems for learning in pluralistic settings. One approach to preaching does not fit all. Yet a course simply surveying all of the homiletical possibilities available will not provide a foundation on which to build either.

Furthermore, while there are numerous introductory preaching textbooks from which to choose, most are written from the perspective of Euro-American males. Classes supplement this view with smaller homiletical texts written by women and persons of color. But a pedagogical hierarchy is nevertheless set up: the white male voice provides the main course and women and persons of color provide the side dishes.

Elements of Preaching is a series designed to help professors and students of preaching—including established preachers who want to develop their skills in specific areas—construct a sound homiletical foundation in a conversational manner. This conversation is meant to occur at two levels. First, the series as a whole deals with basic components found in most introductory preaching classes: theology of proclamation, homiletical contexts, biblical interpretation, sermonic claim, language and imagery, rhetorical form, delivery, and worship. But each element is presented by a different scholar, all of whom represent diversity in terms of gender, theological traditions (Baptist, Disciple of Christ, Lutheran, Presbyterian, and United Methodist), and ethnicity (African American, Asian American, and Euro-American). Instead of bringing in different voices at the margin of the preaching class, Elements of Preaching creates a conversation around the central topics of an introductory course without foregoing essential instruction concerning sermon construction and embodiment. Indeed, this level of conversation is extended beyond the printed volumes through the Web site www.ElementsofPreaching.com.

Second, the individual volumes are written in an open-ended manner. The individual author's particular views are offered but in a way that invites, indeed demands, the readers to move beyond them in developing their own approaches to the preaching task. The volumes offer theoretical and practical insights, but at the last page it is clear that more must be said. Professors and students have a solid place to begin, but there is flexibility within the class (and after the class in ministry) to move beyond these volumes by building on the insights and advice they offer.

In this volume, Ronald J. Allen surveys the range of theological voices found in the church and academy that are available to the preacher in a post-Enlightenment world. *Thinking Theologically* pushes readers to locate themselves within this spectrum, recognize the strengths and weaknesses of their theological positions, and explore the implications of their worldview for the task of preaching. Too often we preachers preach out of habit—sermons have simply always been part of Christian worship. By critically reflecting on why (the theology *of* preaching) and what (the theology *in* preaching) we are doing, we preachers will be better equipped to offer our congregations the gospel with a voice that is true to our particular engagement with and living out of the Christian faith. Allen's survey helps us begin this process and at the same time leads us to an appreciation of the authenticity of other voices speaking out of their theological locations.

O. Wesley Allen Jr.

Introduction

Theologies today fall into relatively distinct families according to assumptions, sources, purposes, and methods. This book invites preachers to name the particular theological families that inform them, to consider the outcomes for preaching, and to think critically about that family's strengths and limitations in relationship to preaching. This book focuses not on theologies *of* preaching but on how different theological households *shape* preaching.

Part 1 sketches the broad background within which contemporary theological discussion of preaching takes place. Part 2 highlights theological families that extend or nuance Enlightenment emphases (liberal, revisionary, and process theologies). Part 3 considers movements that react against the Enlightenment in different ways (evangelical, Barthian neoorthodox, postliberal, and other theologies). Part 4 discusses theological movements that start not with the Enlightenment but with social context (liberation and ethnic theologies).

Chapters 4 through 12 follow the same pattern: a broad outline of the theological house and its purposes for preaching, a case study of how preachers might interpret the same biblical text—Jesus raising the child of the widow of Nain (Luke 7:11-17), and questions raised by that theological family. Each chapter includes a short list of readings that are representative of the subject of that chapter.

Using This Book

Many preachers will read the following descriptions and think, "I do not belong exclusively to one theological family. My approach to preaching contains elements from different theological houses." In fact, my work on this book helped me realize that many of these boundaries are artificial. A scholar of preaching corresponding with me regarding the categories of this project wrote: "A most interesting list, but I am not sure I appear on your list." This scholar self-identified as a sacramental preacher in the Anglican tradition with impulses toward mutual critical correlation and radical orthodoxy. Indeed, many books on preaching do not fit neatly into one theological category but embrace elements from different theological families. In the Representative Readings sections, I have listed works whose theological perspectives are fairly distinct. I have not listed many books that mix theological categories. Of course, these lists are *representative* and not exhaustive.

Nevertheless, while some preachers draw on multiple theological families, most preachers do have *a center of theological gravity*. That is, most preachers settle into one of these families more than others. A minister's approach to preaching is usually a little more closely related to one family than to others. I hope this book will help preachers name their centering points so they then can self-consciously and critically build on its strengths and address its weaknesses, cognizant of what is gained and lost and of how their approach fits into the larger theological world.

Throughout the book I speak as if the preacher always bases the sermon on the exposition of a particular biblical text. However, preachers sometimes preach not on particular biblical passages but on biblical themes, or on Christian doctrines or theological motifs, or on Christian practices, or on personal or social situations. The reader can transfer remarks in this book focused on preaching on biblical passages to other kinds of preaching.[1]

The Biblical Text Used as Illustration

Since the chapters in the heart of the book comment on how different theological families might interpret Luke 7:11-17, the NRSV text is printed here. Prior to this reading Jesus was in Capernaum and had just healed the servant of a Roman centurion (Luke 7:1-10).

> [11]Soon afterwards, he [Jesus] went to a town called Nain, and his disciples and a large crowd went with him. [12]As he approached the gate of the town, a man who had died was being carried out. He was his mother's only son, and she was a widow; and with her was a large crowd from the town. [13]When the Lord saw her, he had compassion for her and said to her, "Do not weep." [14]Then he came forward and touched the bier, and the bearers stood still. And he said, "Young man, I say to you, rise!" [15]The dead man sat up and began to speak, and Jesus gave him to his mother. [16]Fear seized all of them; and they glorified God saying, "A great prophet has risen among us," and "God has looked favorably upon [these] people!" [17]This word about him spread throughout Judea and all the surrounding countryside.

Acknowledgments

I express appreciation to several people who read pieces of earlier versions of this book: Charles W. Allen, David Bundy, Charles L. Campbell, Sergius Halversen, Lucy Lind Hogan, John C. Holbert, Michael Monshau, David Schnasa Jacobsen, David Lose, John S. McClure, John C. Holbert, Robert S. Reid, Timothy Warren, Dawn Ottoni Wilhelm, and Douglas Gwyn. The observations of O. Wesley Allen Jr., editor of this series, were seminal in conceiving and reconceiving this project.

PART ONE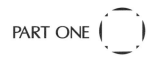

Theology and Preaching
Background to Contemporary Approaches

A computer user can easily see programs identified by icons on the main screen that are activated by a single click. Much less obvious are programs running in the background whose icons may be miniatures at the bottom of the screen or may not appear on the screen at all. Nevertheless, background programs affect how the computer operates by doing such things as providing instant access to the programs, allowing other programs to link together, or even blocking such connections. Before I learned about programs running in the background, I once had so many going invisibly that they slowed my computer to the point that I could go to the kitchen and prepare a meal while the programs switched from one task to another.

Certain theological factors are much like background programs running in the preacher's approach to the sermon. Part 1 examines three factors often running in the preacher's background. Chapter 1 focuses on the preacher's theological convictions as a lens between the preacher and the biblical text. The preacher's theology often prompts the preacher to see some things and to be less aware of others. Chapter 2 focuses on historic Christian movements that often provide the preacher with background theological orientations. Chapter 3 summarizes chief lines of the Enlightenment. Many contemporary approaches to preaching are continuing responses to the Enlightenment, either refining Enlightenment perspectives or reacting against them. Of particular importance to contemporary theology and preaching is the work of the German theologian Friedrich Schleiermacher.

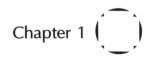

Chapter 1

Theology Shapes Preaching

At the beginning of preaching class, I ask students how they understand the purpose of preaching. Usually most students say the minister aims "to preach the Bible." However, in the same way that glasses sit between my eyes and the rest of the world, the preacher's theology sits between the preacher and the sermon. The preacher does not simply preach the Bible but interprets the Bible through a theological lens.

What Is Theology?

The word *theology* comes from two Greek words that mean "thinking about" (Gk.: *logos*) and "God" (*theos*). In the general sense each Christian has a theology because each Christian thinks about God. My colleague Helene Russell points out that most Christians have an embedded theology, that is, an approach to theological beliefs and issues that they take for granted. Some embedded theology is intuitive and never rises to the level of explicit awareness. In a more explicit sense, however, theology refers to the systematic attempt to state as clearly as possible the deepest convictions of a particular Christian or Christian community.

Whether informal or formal, whether embedded or the result of critical development, theology assumes or sets forth what the community most deeply believes about the following:[1]

- The resources and means whereby human beings come to an interpretation of God—for instance, revelation, Bible, tradition, experience, the arts and sciences, human interpretation—

4

especially what preachers and congregations believe about the relationship of God and the Bible;

- God, especially God's nature and character, the purposes of God for human life and for the natural world, the extent of God's power and how it operates, and what God offers and asks;

- Jesus Christ, especially the relationship of Christ to God and the Holy Spirit, the nature and work of Christ as a part of the work of God, and the relationship of Christ to Judaism;

- The Holy Spirit, especially the relationship of the Spirit to God and Christ, the nature and work of the Spirit, the purposes of the Spirit as well as the manifestation, experience, and leading of the Spirit;

- The church, especially the nature and purpose of the church, the relationship of different Christian communities to one another and the relationship of the church to other communities in the world, the essential marks of the church, how to understand defining practices internal to the church (such as baptism, the sacred meal, and foot washing), and how to be in mission external to the Christian community;

- The human being (theological anthropology), especially what it means for human beings to be made in the image of God, what it is possible for human beings to know or interpret concerning God's purpose for them, the degree to which human beings can fulfill the purposes of God for human life, the meaning and consequences of sin, how human beings relate to God and to one another as individuals and as communities, the meaning of salvation, what the preacher assumes about listeners and about what can happen when human beings (as individuals and communities) hear a sermon;

- The world (the intertwined relationships of humankind, animals, and the physical environment), especially the degree to which the world in its present state coheres with God's purposes, and eschatology.

The preacher's beliefs about these things (and others), whether informal or formal, implicit or explicit, naïvely embedded or critically developed, affects the way the preacher understands the Bible and what the preacher expects to find in the Bible. The preacher should try to name how these things affect the preacher's own theological thinking as well as the similar factors that are at work in the congregation. The preacher can then reflect critically on how these qualities play positively and negatively into how the preacher develops the sermon and in how the congregation receives it. The preacher's theological ideas further shape how the preacher understands the congregation as a listening community, and what the preacher regards as the goal of the sermon.

Each preacher's theological approach to the sermon contains elements that are particular to that preacher.[2] However, preachers seldom create a theology of preaching entirely from one theological house but tend to draw from broader families of thought combining elements from historic and contemporary emphases. Each theological household has its own distinctive point of view on God, humankind, church, and world, as well as its own strengths and weaknesses. Yet no one approach to preaching resolves every issue. Indeed, given human finitude, we never can achieve full theological knowledge. Even our best and most complete theological utterances are partial. Preachers need to make critically informed choices among theologies regarding issues and questions with which preachers are most willing to live. The relationships among preacher, text, theology, and sermon are represented in diagram 1.

Diagram 1 — A Circular Relationship
Preacher, Text, Theological Perspectives, and Sermon

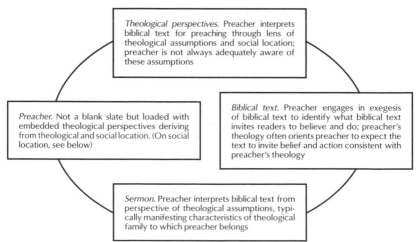

Diagram 1 pictures traffic flowing among the biblical text, the preacher, the preacher's theological perspectives, and the sermon. A preacher's theology is seldom static and unchanging but usually evolves in response to fresh data, questions, and life events. Indeed, a preacher's encounter with a biblical text can cause the preacher to rethink aspects of theology. A preacher, for instance, may encounter a biblical text that prompts the preacher to recognize that her or his perspective on justice is too limited.

The preacher does not simply preach the text but interprets the biblical text (or a theme, doctrine, practice, or issue) through the lens of the preacher's theological assumptions (deepest convictions about God, Christ, Holy Spirit, church, and world) and social location. At the same time, the Bible influences the preacher's theological perspectives and understanding of the purpose of the sermon. The more preachers can be aware of the lenses through which we develop sermons, the more we can think critically about how to enhance the strengths of our lenses and how to account for the weaknesses.

Other Factors That Affect the Preacher's Approach to the Sermon

Because of its limited size and clearly focused agenda, this book concentrates on the relationship between theology and preaching. However, contemporary theologians are increasingly aware that the preacher's social location often plays an important role in forming the preacher's theology and approach to the sermon. Factors such as the following contribute to a preacher's social location:

- Ethnicity

- Gender

- Social class

- Values of local community

- Political commitments

- Educational level

- Philosophical school

- Gender orientation

- National experience (for instance, as colony or imperial power)

North American preachers of European origin tend to take their social locations for granted and even to assume that their privileges are normative for other peoples. With respect to ethnicity, for instance, many Eurocentric preachers are only dimly aware of the struggles of African Americans, Hispanics, Asian Americans and Native Americans. Males tend to read texts (and to think theologically) in ways that support male dominance and that subordinate women.

The preacher can be helped in two ways by developing awareness of the preacher's social location. (1) Preachers (especially those of European origin) can be critical of ways that their social locations prematurely foreclose interpretive options. As a member of the middle class, for instance, I tend to interpret texts in ways that help the congregation pursue comfortable middle-class values and lifestyles. When I become aware of this interpretive tendency, I can be more open to biblical texts that invite me to consider possibilities for social transformation. (2) Preachers can use their social locations as points of contact and identification with the biblical text. For example, a preacher from a marginalized community that has an essentially communal sense of identity might be sensitive not only to the communal element assumed by people in the world of the Bible but also might perceive the need for the relationships among different communities in North America to become more egalitarian in order better to reflect God's purposes.

The list of factors forming a preacher's social location is almost endless, ranging from experiences in the preacher's family of origin to international events that affect social stability and that generate feelings. Even if preachers cannot take complete account of the qualities that influence their social locations, preachers can identify the main ones.

Representative Readings

Allen, Ronald J. *Preaching and Practical Ministry.* Preaching and Its Partners. St. Louis: Chalice, 2001. Preaching in congregational systems with attention to teaching, counseling, administration, mission, spirituality

———. "The Preacher as Philosopher." *Quarterly Review* 1, no. 2 (1997): 87–111. Preaching in relationship to philosophy.

Childers, Jana, ed. *Purposes of Preaching.* St. Louis: Chalice, 2004. Ten scholars of preaching set out ten different understandings of preaching in theological terms.

Cooper, Burton Z., and John S. McClure, *Claiming Theology in the Pulpit.* Louisville: Westminster John Knox, 2003. Helps preachers analyze theological convictions according to key categories.

Duke, Robert. *The Sermon as God's Word: Theologies for Preaching.* Abingdon Preacher's Library. Nashville: Abingdon, 1980. Explores Barth, Tillich, liberalism, fundamentalism, and black liberation theology.

Luck, Donald. *Why Study Theology?* St. Louis: Chalice, 1999. A primer on the importance of theology, goals of theology, critical thinking.

McKim, Donald. *The Bible in Theology and Preaching: How Preachers Use Scripture.* Nashville: Abingdon, 1985. Fourteen theological families and their views of Scripture.

Stone, Howard W., and James D. Duke, *How to Think Theologically.* 2nd ed. Minneapolis: Fortress Press, 2006. Relationship of theology to faith, resources for thinking theologically, theological method, the gospel, human condition, vocation, community as context, spiritual formation.

Wilson, Paul Scott. *Preaching and Homiletical Theory.* Preaching and Its Partners. St. Louis: Chalice, 2004. Contemporary preaching theories from perspective of theological grounding, claims, and implications.

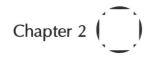
Historic Theologies Still Shape Preaching

Most of this book focuses on how contemporary theologies shape preaching (chaps. 4–12). These viewpoints often cross denominational lines. For instance, liberation theologians are found in churches as diverse as Roman Catholic, Lutheran, Baptist, and Pentecostal. In addition, theologies that originated in the past (and are often associated with particular denominations) contribute to how preachers understand the sermon in many different traditions. For example, my approach to theology and preaching is Reformed as refracted through the Christian Church (Disciples of Christ), while also in conversation with process theology and with my social location as a middle-class, privileged male of European descent who is influenced by liturgical theological developments from the Second Vatican Council of the Roman Catholic Church (see below).

To continue the analogy of computer programs whose icons are on the main screen with programs running in the background (p. 3), historical theologies are sometimes on the main screen, but are sometimes in the background. This chapter summarizes leading themes pertaining to preaching in ten historic theological families in the hope that readers will think critically about how motifs from their historic traditions interact with the orientation of their contemporary theological influences. Combinations of historical and contemporary movements are summarized in table 2 in the reprise (p. 90).

Orthodox

While the Orthodox Church is large and diverse—consisting of several self-governing and ethnically distinct bodies—the belief that the service of worship has sacramental qualities is at the core of Orthodox Christianity. Indeed, the Orthodox understand their liturgy as an opportunity for people on earth to experience a measure of heaven, a foretaste of union with the divine that will be complete and everlasting only after death when self and community are forever in the heavenly world. Icons—one of the distinctive features of the Orthodox churches—are not idols but function as windows to heaven that allow the light of heaven to pour into the world and, indeed, into the hearts of those who contemplate them. At one level, the sermon performs a teaching function by instructing the congregation in what happens in worship as well as in the basic tenets of doctrine and ethical behavior. At another level, the sermon can have a sacramental quality. The experience of hearing the sermon can be a moment when the congregation's perception is elevated into the heavenly realm. The sermon both interprets that realm and is a medium of the experience of that realm. We might call the sermon an oral-aural icon, as it is a means through which the incarnate Word of God becomes present.

Roman Catholic

The Second Vatican Council of the Roman Catholic Church (1963–65) initiated one of the most influential trajectories in worship and preaching in the past fifty years. Prior to Vatican II (as that council is popularly called), Roman Catholic preachers typically conceived of the sermon as an exposition of Catholic belief. While the Bible was always read during the Mass (the liturgy or service of worship), the preacher sometimes gave little attention to the Bible and concentrated on imparting Catholic doctrine, regulating ethical behavior, and encouraging personal devotions.

Although the Second Vatican Council did not officially declare preaching to be a sacrament, the Constitution on the Sacred Liturgy states that Christ is truly present not only in the loaf and the cup but also in the congregation and in the sermon.[1] In the vivid expression of Mary Catherine Hilkert, the preacher is to "name grace" as it is present in the Scriptures, in the service of worship, in the life of the church, and in the broader world.[2] Moreover, there is a sense in which the sermon itself mediates grace.

An important document inspired by Vatican II, *Fulfilled in Your Hearing* (published by the Bishops' Committee on Priestly Life and Ministry of the United States Conference of Catholic Bishops), plays a key role in shaping preaching in the Roman Catholic Church today.[3] The bishops call for sermons with the following qualities. (1) The preacher is to base the sermon on the Scriptures while keeping church doctrine in mind. (2) The preacher is to be guided by the Christian year and is to develop sermons from texts found in the lectionary. This movement reinforces the use of lectionaries organized on the principle of *lectio selecta*—selecting Bible readings from different parts of the Bible to fit the theological themes associated with the seasons and days of the Christian year: Advent, Christmas, Epiphany, Lent, Easter, Pentecost, and Ordinary Time. (3) The preacher is to speak more in the indicative than the imperative, that is, the preacher announces what God does for salvation more than tells people how to live. (4) The preacher is to speak in the everyday language of the congregation and not in theological abstractions. Finally, this document encourages preachers to use their own lives as lenses through which to refract the gospel.

Prior to Vatican II, many Protestant preachers developed topical sermons that gave scant attention to the Bible and theology. However, several Protestant denominations joined the Second Vatican Council in recognizing the theological values of developing sermons from a selected lectionary in the context of the Christian year. The most commonly used lectionary in North America today, the Revised Common Lectionary, was generated in response to the liturgical reforms of Vatican II.[4] This movement now includes many congregations that are Lutheran, Episcopal, Presbyterian, Reformed, United Methodist, Christian Church (Disciples of Christ), United Church of Christ, Baptist, and Anabaptist.

Anglican and Episcopalian

Since the Anglican and Episcopalian churches are closely related in some key respects to the Roman Catholic Church, it is not surprising that their understanding of preaching runs in a sacramental stream. Christ is present through the words of the sermon in a way similar to the real presence in the bread and the cup. The sermon typically derives from a passage from the Revised Common Lectionary and takes account of the Eucharist and the liturgical season and Sunday of the Christian year. Major purposes of the sermon include helping the congregation discover how the biblical material and broader church teaching lead the congregation to make theological sense of the world. The preacher often describes how the Bible readings and other theological resources encourage the community to recognize and respond to the real presence. The sermon contains a teaching element while also becoming the medium through which the congregation can experience the real presence through the words of the preacher.

Lutheran

Lutherans prescribe preaching from the Bible, typically as organized by the Revised Common Lectionary and the Christian year. Central to Lutheran theology is the conviction that Christ is truly present in the sermon (in the same way that Christ is truly present in the sacrament). Since God is a speaking God, God speaks when the preacher speaks. Given the prominence of law and gospel in Lutheran theology, preachers often bring these two motifs into the sermon. The law makes people painfully aware of sin and our inability to effect our own salvation. The preaching of the law should create a profound longing to hear the gospel (the news that God justifies human beings by grace through Jesus Christ). A major function of the sermon is to help the community accept the love of God for sinners manifest through Christ. Indeed, many Lutheran sermons are structured as movement from law to grace, from acknowledgment of sin to awareness of God's unmerited favor. The sermon often guides the community in responding to that grace. Martin Luther thought of the pulpit as a battlefield through which God confronts Satan and the demons. Lutherans are especially tenacious in naming works righteousness as a manifestation of sin and in calling attention to God's grace as the only resolution to the human struggle to justify ourselves.

Reformed

The Reformed churches have one of the clearest understandings of preaching for, following John Calvin, they think of the sermon as teaching event. Starting with a Bible passage, the Reformed sermon helps the congregation identify how God is gracious, how that grace is still at work in the world, and how grace helps the congregation respond in faith. Calvin cautions that neither the biblical words nor the preacher's words are automatically God's words; the work of the Holy Spirit must give the sermon the quality of becoming God's word. As noted previously Luther regarded the function of the law as making human beings aware of sin and of their need for the gospel. Calvin identified another function of the law, namely to guide the congregation in the ways of God. Reformed preaching, then, often includes a function that is similar to Calvin's additional understanding of the law in that the preacher attempts to teach the congregation how to live faithfully. Until recently Reformed preachers had a proclivity for *lectio contina* (continuous reading)—that is, preaching from start to finish through a biblical book (or other large part of the Bible)—but today many Reformed preachers follow the Revised Common Lectionary. Reformed approaches to preaching occur today in the various Presbyterian communions, the Reformed Church, wings of the United Church of Christ, and in the Christian Church (Disciples of Christ), the Christian Churches affiliated with the North American Christian Convention, and the Churches of Christ.

Wesleyan

The *raison d'etre* of Wesleyan preaching is captured in an expression of John Wesley as "plain truth for plain people."[5] At the time of Wesley, many sermons in the established church were flowery and complex. Wesley thought such preaching ostentatious. Consequently, Wesley preached in a simple way in the confidence that the Holy Spirit would work with the preacher and the congregation to bring about awareness of God's love. Indeed, the heart of Wesleyan theology is captured in one of the distinctive hymns of this movement, which asserts that God is "pure unbounded love."[6] The heart of Wesleyan preaching, then, is to help the listening community become aware of their need for God and to recognize Christ as manifestation of God's love for them. Wesleyan preaching further aims to guide the congregation in the way of sanctification or holiness. That is, the preacher seeks to help the congregation grow in its ability to live a holy life, a life that demonstrates God's desires in personal and corporate life. Members of the congregation choose whether to accept this love. In line with Wesleyan theology, sermons in this tradition often emphasize repentance, justification by grace, and holiness. A Wesleyan flavor in preaching is often found in the African Methodist Episcopal Church, the African Methodist Episcopal Zion Church, the Christian Methodist Episcopal Church, the United Methodist Church, the Nazarene Church, and other Wesleyan and Holiness communions.

Anabaptist

The Anabaptist churches are descended from the *radical reformation* of the Swiss, Dutch, and German reformers of the sixteenth century and are known today as Amish, Mennonites, Hutterites, and Brethren. These communities are noted for their distinct practices of public worship and preaching and their commitment to keep separate from worldly values and behaviors. Preaching is intended to inspire faith and to help the congregation as community to embody the realm of God as an alternative to the present world. These churches look to the Bible as the main source of theological guidance. Enlivened by the Spirit, the sermon becomes an expression of God's word for the listening community. Preachers sometimes follow the free selection of texts or continuous lectionary, though increasingly the Christian Year and a selected lectionary is followed. Preachers in the radical wing of the Reformation tend to regard the message as an instrument to help the established community grow in discipleship. The Anabaptist emphasis on the priesthood of all believers leads some congregations to follow the sermon with a period in which members of the congregation give their interpretations of the biblical text, respond to the sermon, and offer testimony. Such reflections often are, effectively, a continuation of the sermon.

Another group of separatists, similar to the Anabaptists, emerged from the Church of England during the seventeenth century and today meet under the *Baptist* name. These churches exhibit considerable variety in theology and styles of worship. Most Baptists place a high priority on the notion that preachers are called and inspired by the Spirit to deliver a message to the congregation. The Baptist sermon typically assumes that "all are guilty and fall short of the glory of God," and, therefore, every individual is accountable before God "without the imposition of creed, the interference of clergy, or the intervention of civil government."[7] A common expression for this phenomenon in Baptist circles is "soul freedom." Of course, individuals must accept the grace of God revealed through Jesus Christ and respond to that grace in the whole spectrum of life. Sermons tend either to be structured in ways that persuasively move toward an invitation to repent, to commit to the big idea of the sermon, or to the action the sermon seeks. Though issue-oriented or topical preaching occurs, expository preaching of biblical texts dominates this tradition. Many preachers freely select a biblical passage while others preach sequentially through parts of the Bible (*lectio continua*) and some follow the Christian year and a selected lectionary. Such preaching is found in the many Baptist conventions, for example, American, Cooperative Baptist Fellowship, Independent, Missionary, National, Progressive, Progressive Missionary, Southern, and others.

Society of Friends

The best-known aspect of the Friends is their reliance upon silence in worship and upon the movement of the Spirit in the congregation to lead members to rise and speak out of the silence. Many Friends believe that the risen Jesus teaches the community using the words of those who are called to rise and speak. Some services of worship are altogether unprogrammed: the community gathers in silence and waits for the Spirit to move. Many other meetings (congregations) are programmed, that is, they have an order of worship that includes both silence and a sermon. George Fox, the founder of the Friends, was a well-known preacher. The preacher names the grace of God and helps the community reflect on divine leading. When the message responds to the leading of the Spirit, the message becomes a means through which the risen Jesus continues to teach the people. Many meetings are semi-programmed, meaning that a brief order of worship is prepared ahead of time (which generally includes a sermon) followed by silence and the opportunity for other members of the meeting to rise and speak as are led by the Spirit of Christ.

Pentecostal

While the Pentecostal movement is only a little more than a hundred years old, it is a distinct and fast-growing tradition. Pentecostal preachers are usually evangelical in orientation and emphasize the presence and work of the Holy Spirit. Pentecostals think the Spirit fills individuals and congregations with ecstatic awareness of the presence of God that sometimes is expressed by speaking in tongues and dramatic manifestations but also can be expressed quietly. Indeed, the present experience of the Spirit anticipates the final manifestation of the Spirit in the eschatological age. Pentecostals believe that the Holy Spirit anoints the preacher. Some ministers in this tradition do not prepare the sermon because they believe that the Spirit will speak through them spontaneously in the moment of preaching. Most Pentecostal ministers, however, are confident that the Spirit can inspire the preacher during preparation as well as during preaching. The Spirit also prompts the congregation to receive the message. While Pentecostal sermons emphasize God's grace through Christ, their distinctive emphasis is on the prophetic, empowering, liberating work of the Spirit. The Pentecostal sermon expects that the community will use the gifts of the Spirit. Churches associated with this movement in North America include the Apostolic Churches, Assemblies of God, Church of God (Cleveland, Tennessee), Church of God in Christ, International Church of the Foursquare Gospel, Pentecostal Assemblies of the World, United Pentecostal Church, more than three hundred additional Pentecostal associations, and many independent local congregations.

Historical and Contemporary Theologies Often Come Together in Preaching

Themes from these historical perspectives are seldom immediately evident in the discussions of the contemporary theological families that follow. Yet motifs from the historical trajectories often surface in the sermon, especially when the preacher interprets particular doctrines or practices such as baptism, the sacred meal, or the purposes of the church and of preaching.

Representative Readings

Edwards, O. C. Jr. *A History of Preaching.* Nashville: Abingdon, 2004. Effervescent telling of the story of the history of preaching; accompanied by a CD-ROM containing illustrative sermons.

González, Justo L., and Pablo A. Jiménez. *Púlpito: An Introduction to Hispanic Preaching.* Nashville: Abingdon, 2005. Major trends in Hispanic preaching, especially Protestant, in the last two hundred years.

Kienzle, Marilyn B., and Pamela J. Walker, eds. *Women Prophets and Preachers through Two Millennia of Christianity.* Berkeley: University of California Press, 1998. Women in the pulpit and other positions of leadership.

Kim, Eunjoo Mary. *Women Preaching: Theology and Practice Through the Ages.* Cleveland: Pilgrim, 2004. Women and preaching with attention to Asian American heritage.

LaRue, Cleophus J. *The Heart of Black Preaching.* Louisville: Westminster John Knox, 1999. Key themes and figures in African American preaching.

Mitchell, Henry H. *Black Preaching: Recovery of a Powerful Art.* Nashville: Abingdon, 1990. Formative motifs in African American preaching.

McClain, William B. *Come Sunday: The Liturgy of Zion.* Nashville: Abingdon, 1990. African American preaching and worship with interest in Wesleyan tradition.

Old, Hughes Oliphant. *The Reading and Preaching of the Scriptures in the Worship of the Christian Church.* 6 vols. Grand Rapids: Eerdmans, 1998, 1998, 1999, 2002, 2004, 2006. Reformed perspective on history of preaching.

Osborn, Ronald E. *Folly of God: The Rise of Christian Preaching.* A History of Christian Preaching. St. Louis: Chalice, 1999. Vol. 1, through the third century C.E. Joseph R. Jeter Jr. is preparing volume 2.

Mountford, Roxanne. *The Gendered Pulpit: Preaching in American Protestant Spaces.* Carbondale: Southern Illinois University Press, 2005. Influence of gender.

Wilson, Paul Scott. *A Concise History of Preaching.* Nashville: Abingdon, 1992. Thumbnail sketches of major figures in history of preaching illustrated by excerpts from sermons.

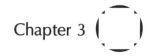

Chapter 3

The Enlightenment
Backdrop to Many Contemporary Theologies and Preaching

Historians and philosophers often divide the intellectual history of people of European origin into three great intellectual periods. Scholars date the premodern period as beginning with the dawn of civilization and lasting until the Enlightenment (eighteenth century), the modern period as extending from the Enlightenment into the late twentieth century, and the postmodern era as beginning in the late twentieth century and continuing in the new millennium.[1] In this chapter we focus on premodern and modern perspectives while giving more attention to postmodernism in the chapters on mutual critical correlation, process thought, postliberalism, and other theologies,

In general speech the word *modern* is often a synonym for "contemporary" and means "up-to-date." In theological discourse, however, the term *modern* refers specifically to the worldview emanating from the Enlightenment. Expressions such as "modern theology" or "modern preaching" refer to theology and preaching characterized by Enlightenment concerns.

Premodern Perception

In premodern communities tradition often is the primary source of authority, meaning, and purpose. People tend to assume that the values of the tradition provide reliable guidance for life, and people often frown on those who depart from tradition. Premodern societies understand human identity in terms of communal belonging and not as something that individuals achieve on their own. The self, in premodern terms, is a self-in-community whose highest goals include being faithful to community values and contributing to the community as a whole. People understand themselves always to represent the community and understand the community to be present through them. Many people in the premodern world believe in the presence of supra-human entities—God or gods, and beings such as angels, demons, and other kinds of spirits. Furthermore, such people often imagine that these supra-human beings play important roles in controlling the world and in the lives of communities, households, and individuals. A common belief is that such powers can take a direct role in human affairs and in nature. Premodern groups sometimes anthropomorphize supra-human beings—for instance, speaking of God as if God were a giant person who walks and talks and causes events on the earth and in the heavens by gesturing with the divine hand. Some premoderns think that elements of nature are animated. While these folk do not think animals and rocks have personality in the same sense as a person, they often imagine elements in the cosmos as responsive to the will of the gods.

In a premodern religious community, the preacher passes the content of the tradition from generation to generation and explains how to understand new circumstances from its perspective. The preacher helps people discern how to live in harmony with the gods so that the community can have a full and secure life. People within a community may disagree on how to interpret tradition, but the validity of tradition itself is seldom questioned.

The Enlightenment and the Modern Worldview

The Enlightenment, whose roots are in the Renaissance and the Age of Reason, gave birth to two related motifs. First is the rise of the scientific method, which refers to the idea that people can accept as true and trustworthy only those things that have been confirmed by empirical observation, that is, by the five senses. Second, a companion movement in philosophy, called rationalism, sought "logically unchallenged first truths."[2] Thinkers would reason from such foundational principles, or first principles, to their implications.

A goal of Enlightenment thinking was to establish truths that were universally valid. Using the scientific method or beginning from first principles, modern philosophers and theologians sought to identify ideas that are true in every time and place. Using these criteria, Enlightenment thinkers charged that many premodern views could not be trusted because many premodern traditions describe events, perspectives, or possibilities that cannot be verified by scientific observation or by deduction from first principles. Some presumptions of premodernism contradict good scientific or philosophical thinking. Indeed, tradition is often arbitrary and authoritarian in ways that misdirect and even crush the human spirit.

Of particular interest to preachers are Enlightenment attitudes toward history and the divine. In the premodern setting the community trusted in tradition. From an Enlightenment perspective the purpose of the discipline of history is to determine what was objectively true in the past. Tradition could be considered dependable only when its depiction of reality was confirmed through empirical or philosophical investigation. Consistent with their emphasis on empirical observation as the primary mode of gathering knowledge, Enlightenment historians and philosophers aimed to achieve pure, unbiased, objective understanding of texts (ancient and contemporary texts) and, indeed, all other phenomena. This Enlightenment emphasis is the root of the historical criticism that most preachers today learn in seminary.

These perspectives caused many Enlightenment advocates to dismiss a fair number of texts from the Bible and even to reject the idea of God, since the existence and activity of a deity cannot be proven through typical scientific observation or philosophical deduction. The questions raised by the Enlightenment regarding the trustworthiness of biblical texts, traditional Christian doctrines, and even about the possibility of God's existence were sometimes called "the acids of modernity" because they seemed to eat away the community's confidence in many of the assertions of the Bible and of Christian doctrine.

The Enlightenment brought other changes to premodern consciousness. Many people began to conceive of human identity as less communal and more individualistic. The Enlightenment, as part of wider impulses associated with the industrial revolution, tended to view the natural world less as a partner with humankind and more as a commodity that could be manipulated for human benefit.

Schleiermacher: Experience as Central Resource for Theology

With the acids of modernity washing over them, Enlightenment preachers were in a quandary. In a world in which people sought empirical confirmation as the definitive sign of trustworthiness, what could the preacher commend that the community could believe, especially since so much of the Bible and of Christian doctrine asserted things that cannot be investigated by the usual empirical or philosophical means? Friedrich Schleiermacher articulated a response that became the foundation of the liberal movement in theology. Schleiermacher's approach to theology was widely embraced by preachers in his own time and is still alive in some quarters today.

Schleiermacher was on the cusp of the Romantic movement. At that time the term *romantic* referred not to feelings of attraction on the part of one person to another (in the way that I say, "I have romantic feelings for my wife") but bespoke a movement of people who accepted many principles of the Enlightenment but who found it cold, intellectually brittle, and incomplete. The Romantics, in the late eighteenth century, turned to "feeling" as a significant source of awareness.

Schleiermacher lived at a time when many people looked down on religion, concluding that its claims could not be established by reputable means. Some such people regarded religion as little more than superstition. Some people who did turn to religion thought of it as little more than rational reflections on God, with many drifting into deism (the idea that God created the world and then essentially withdrew, letting the world operate according to the laws that God had established). A few people adhered to the idea that the Bible and Christian theology contain truths revealed from God and that the purpose of the church was to continue those assertions even in the face of scientific, philosophical evidences to the contrary.

Schleiermacher articulated an alternative perspective on religion that was sympathetic to the Enlightenment liberation from primitivism and arbitrary authoritarianism but was not sterile like the religion of the rationalists. Schleiermacher offered an approach to religion grounded in actual experience, but the experience of interior feeling. In one of Schleiermacher's most famous books, *On Religion: Speeches to Its Cultured Despisers*,[3] the famous German theologian sought to show that the church can have a lively approach to religion without appealing to a notion of revelation that goes against the grain of the norms of Enlightenment standards for truth.[4] The core of Schleiermacher's vision is that all people have an incipient dimension of religious experience that Schleiermacher described as a *"feeling* of utter dependence" on God.[5] According to Schleiermacher, everyone has this feeling. By "feeling" Schleiermacher means not just emotion but the whole gamut of intuitive awareness. Religion is not simply knowing or doing but involves vital experience that permeates the self. "Religion is to seek this [feeling] and find it in all that lives and moves, in all growth and change, in all doing and suffering. It is to have life and know life in immediate feeling, only as such an existence in the Infinite and Eternal."[6] While Schleiermacher believed that Christianity is the highest expression of religion, he thought that all religions were grounded in deep feeling. Religious practices sought to provide a way for individuals and communities to name their experience and to live in response to it.

Theology and forms of religion, for Schleiermacher, are to help people understand the feeling of dependence and to respond appropriately. Schleiermacher believed that human beings never could fully understand the depths of this feeling, so that an element of mystery is at the deepest point of life. While he thought that Christianity was the highest form of religion, he also thought that other religions attempted to name the feeling of absolute dependence and to prescribe lives consistent with those feelings.

Representative Readings

Allen, Ronald J., Scott Black Johnston, and Barbara Shires Blaisdell. *Theology for Preaching: Authority, Truth, and Knowledge of God in a Postmodern Setting.* Nashville: Abingdon, 1997. Premodern, modern, and postmodern views on authority, truth, knowledge, God, community, and discourse.

DeVries, Dawn. *Jesus Christ in the Preaching of Calvin and Schleiermacher.* Columbia Series in Reformed Theology. Louisville: Westminster John Knox, 2002. Case study of Schleiermacher on preaching Jesus Christ.

Gay, Peter. *The Enlightenment and the Rise of Modern Paganism* and *The Enlightenment: The Rise of Modern Freedom.* New ed. New York: Norton, 1995, 1996 (2 vols.). Classic description of the Enlightenment.

Schleiermacher, Friedrich. *On Religion: Speeches to Its Cultured Despisers.* Ed. Richard Crofter. Cambridge Texts in Religion and Philosophy. Cambridge: Cambridge University Press, 1996.

———. *Selected Sermons of Friedrich Schleiermacher.* Trans. Mary F. Wilson. Eugene: Wipf and Stock, 2004. Sermons showing Schleiermacher's theology in homiletical action.

PART TWO

Theological Movements in the Enlightenment Tradition

We now turn to three theological movements that are broadly in the Enlightenment tradition. Each of these families develops, reshapes, and sometimes even rejects particular elements from the Enlightenment and Schleiermacher. The first theological household discussed, *liberal theology*, seeks to overcome the gap in worldview between the Bible (and historic Christian doctrine) and contemporary conceptions of the world. The approach of liberal theology to preaching offers a clear and direct route from the ancient text to the contemporary congregation. The second theological family—*theology as mutual critical correlation*—seeks to deal not only with differences in worldview but also with differences in perception of morally acceptable behavior and theological vision between antiquity and today. This approach to preaching is much more complicated than that of liberalism because it often involves criticizing aspects of a biblical text on ethical and theological grounds. The third theological family—*process theology* (or *relational theology*, as it sometimes is called)—seeks to resolve many of the Enlightenment's nagging questions as well as ethical issues regarding how to understand God's relationship to evil by reconceiving the nature of reality and the nature and power of God. Many process theologians and preachers employ the method of mutual critical correlation in the service of a process vision.

Chapter 4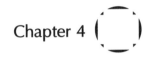

Liberal Theology and Preaching

As noted earlier, some readers may be surprised to find a chapter on liberalism in a book dealing with contemporary theology. The crest of liberal theology took place in the early years of the twentieth century. Some scholars today even speak of liberal theology as naive or passé. However, many ministers in the early twenty-first century continue to interpret the Bible for preaching in ways that are essentially liberal in character.

Liberal Theology in Broad Outline

Liberal thinking in the church typically has two poles. One pole is to help liberate congregations from unenlightened attitudes. Such preachers find core aspects of the Bible and Christian faith to be reliable, but they also conclude that the Bible and traditional Christian doctrine contain elements that are not objectively true. Some of these elements misrepresent reality and move in the direction of superstition. Christians need not subscribe to such beliefs to hold on to the core aspects of Christianity. For many liberals the scientific worldview functioned as a norm by which to measure the credibility of Christian claims. As I once heard someone say, "How can the church ask you to believe something that you otherwise think is not true?"

The other pole of this movement was constructive and aimed to help congregations sort out what they could and could not believe with confidence. Preachers in this tradition typically view the Bible as containing some important clues into what a congregation can (and should) believe and do, but they also recognize that other sources can provide insight. An important point: liberals tend to think that the aspects of the Bible that do not measure up to the best of contemporary understandings of science and history are not essential to Christian faith. Instead, they argue that the Bible contains essential resources to help the church interpret the feeling-awareness at the core of religious life. While the Bible is central to liberal theology, liberals often derive theological inspiration from philosophy, the arts, and the sciences (physical as well as social).

Like Schleiermacher, the later liberal preachers sought a religious faith that is intellectually credible and rich in feeling. We can see this emphasis in the work of Rudolf Bultmann, who represents leading motifs in preaching in the liberal tradition in the early and mid-twentieth century.

In preaching circles, Bultmann is best known for demythologizing the Bible.[1] Bultmann agreed with other liberals that much of the biblical material is cast in premodern, nonscientific, even mythological language, but that beneath the mythological worldview we often encounter an abiding meaning. The mythological language of the Bible is like the husk on an ear of corn. When the farmer removes the husk, the corn itself is exposed. The purpose of the preacher is to demythologize (that is, remove the husk of mythology from a biblical text), identify the abiding theological significance of the text, and then posit what a contemporary community can believe.

Bultmann himself often turned to the philosophical school of existentialism for help in making a positive appropriation of a biblical text. Existentialism claimed that individual human beings determine the character of their existence on the basis of the decisions they make as individuals. While few preachers today follow Bultmann in using existentialism in philosophy as a means to move from the ancient to contemporary worlds, many preachers still engage in forms of demythologizing.

Purposes of Preaching in Liberal Theology

For both Bultmann and for many preachers into the present day, the Bible (and the core of historic Christian tradition) contains two layers of meaning. The surface layer is expressed in ancient worldviews and is cast in historically conditioned language and symbols that no longer speak with immediacy and power to people today. For example, at the time of the Second Testament, many people believed in demons as evil, supra-personal beings who controlled individuals and groups. People in the liberal tradition typically do not believe that such beings exist today.

At the deeper layer, the Bible contains theological perspectives on God and existence (humankind and nature) that are not inherently tied to ancient worldviews or archaic language. The essential task of the preacher is to identify these deeper perspectives and to bring them forward in the sermon. The preacher correlates the message of a biblical passage in its ancient mode of expression with contemporary language and experiences.

Few preachers or scholars of preaching today identify themselves as theological liberals (in the technical sense). Nevertheless, I agree with O. Wesley Allen Jr. who says, "Based on the sermons that I hear and read, I would say that this general approach is the most common hermeneutical method in sermons today."[2] The preacher assumes that the text contains a positive word in the husk of the biblical world. The preacher needs to remove the husk and uncover that word for today.

The preacher *assumes* that a text contains a positive message at the deeper level to guide today's church. If a text appears not to put forward such a message, the preacher probably needs to work harder at understanding its deeper meaning.

This tradition gave birth to a vivid expression for speaking of the differences between ancient and contemporary people: the hermeneutical gap. Preachers often seek to overcome the gap between the ancient and contemporary worlds in one of two ways. In the first approach, preachers seek to extract from a biblical text universal principles that could be valid in any time and place. For example, when faced with a text from the Second Testament asserting that after the resurrection Christ preached to the dead (perhaps in hell), the preacher might regard the abiding message of the text as God's love never giving up but always seeking people, no matter what their circumstances.

The hermeneutic of analogy is a second approach. The preacher seeks to find analogies between the experiences of the ancient and contemporary worlds. Preachers in other theological houses sometimes use this hermeneutic of analogy, especially those who subscribe to process, evangelical, neoorthodox, and postliberal theologies.

The liberal approach often has apologetic dimensions in showing why it is intellectually credible to believe. In the pluralistic religious climate of the early twenty-first century, a liberal approach often offers an alternative to people who want to believe but who are dissatisfied with evangelical and postliberal possibilities. Liberal preaching also has an evangelistic dimension by inviting people who have secular worldviews to consider how they and the cosmos could be enriched by understanding life from a perspective of the transcendent that is at home in their own worldview.

How Liberals Might Interpret Luke 7:11-17

From the larger Lukan perspective, the miracle story functions in several related ways. At the surface level the story demonstrates that Jesus is God's agent in manifesting the Realm of God, that is, in ending the present evil age and bringing about a restored world that fully exhibits God's purposes. In apocalyptic literature death is the most savage enemy of God's realm. Jesus is here a prophet in the tradition of Elijah and Elisha (who performed similar miracles; see, for instance, 1 Kings 17:17-24; 2 Kings 4:18-37). For Luke, the title *prophet* is not a diminution but a fundamental category of interpreting Jesus, especially as apocalyptic prophet. The story embodies God's providence for widows and other vulnerable people. The book of Acts recounts that God continues to raise the dead through the church (for example, Acts 9:36-43, 20:7-12). The story thus represents God's life-giving power for the vulnerable of the world, a power still at work in the church and world since Jesus is resurrected and God has poured out the Holy Spirit on the church to continue the ministry of Jesus. The text is a paradigm for the church in Acts: a community through whom God raises the dead. It is also a paradigm for Luke's own first-century congregation.

A liberal preacher might note that while many people in the ancient world believed that miracles of this kind occurred, a key issue for them was the *significance* of the event. Singular dramatic raisings of the dead (and other miracles) are not a part of our everyday experience. However, a liberal preacher may perceive the deeper aspect of the text, asserting that God continues to manifest care for the vulnerable of the world and that God expresses this concern through Judaism and the church. Indeed, the text suggests that in a world in which many people experience death, the life-giving purposes of God are still at work with a power that death itself cannot extinguish.

From the perspective of the hermeneutic of analogy, the preacher might identify people today who are in situations like the woman and who need not be resigned but can live in hope. Their circumstances may not change through miraculous intervention, but because God is present their worlds are not closed circles. Given the apologetic interest in liberalism, the preacher might point to people today who have been in situations like the widow of Nain—resigned to their circumstances, assuming that they are at a dead end—but for whom, figuratively, the dead are raised.

Questions for Liberal Theology
The largest soft spot in the liberal tradition is the danger of so adapting Christian thinking or action to the contemporary mind-set that the church loses essential marks of Christian identity. When peeling away the surface elements of a text or a historic Christian affirmation, the preacher may strip away the core of the text and set aside elements that are essential to Christian community. I heard someone describe liberal theology as remaking the gospel in the

preacher's own image, with a little pop psychology on the side. However, such difficulties are *not inherent* to liberal theology. While careless practitioners easily can drift in such directions, at its best a liberal approach preserves the core of Christian vision in a compelling way for today's world. Liberal preaching also faces the question of what to do, theologically, with biblical texts that depict God acting (or commanding others to act) in ways that contradict the preacher's deepest convictions concerning God's nature and purposes.

Representative Readings

Allen, Ronald J. *Contemporary Biblical Interpretation for Preaching.* 128–31. Valley Forge: Judson, 1984. Includes the hermeneutic of analogy.

Childers, Jana. *Performing the Word: Preaching as Theater.* Nashville: Abingdon, 1998. Insights into preaching drawn from the world of drama in largely liberal perspective.

Dorrien, Gary. *The Making of American Liberal Theology: Imagining Progressive Religion 1805–1900.* Louisville: Westminster John Knox, 2001. First volume in an excellent trilogy sketching the liberal movement.

———. *The Making of American Liberal Theology: Idealism, Realism, and Modernity 1900–1950.* Louisville: Westminster John Knox, 2003. Second volume in Dorrien's trilogy.

———. *The Making of American Liberal Theology: Crisis, Irony, and Postmodernity.* Louisville: Westminster John Knox, 2006. Third volume in trilogy.

Farris, Stephen. *Preaching That Matters: The Bible and Our Lives.* Louisville: Westminster John Knox, 1998. Though he himself is neoorthodox, Farris gives an excellent description of the hermeneutic of analogy.

Ward, Richard F. *Speaking from the Heart: Preaching with Passion.* Nashville: Abingdon, 1992. Sees the preacher as largely reperforming the text.

———. *Speaking of the Holy: The Art of Communication in Preaching.* St. Louis: Chalice, 2001. An approach to preaching, storytelling, and public presentation of the Bible (reading, recitation, retelling) from perspective of performance theory.

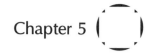

Chapter 5

Theology of Mutual Critical Correlation and Preaching

The language of "correlation" in contemporary theology is most associated with Paul Tillich, who sought to correlate present issues and experience with biblical texts.[1] The preacher begins with questions about contemporary issues and then turns to the biblical text for answers. Tillich thought that the significance of the text must be translated into the present. Tillich thought that in its original contexts the language of the Bible and of formative Christian tradition were key religious symbols that evoked a vital experience of the realities to which they pointed. For Tillich, the realities to which the biblical and traditional symbols pointed are still present today. Over time, however, the biblical and historic language of the Christian community has lost much of its power to evoke the living experience that it had in earlier times. Tillich proposed, therefore, the theological method of correlation, which, as its name suggests, sought to correlate the experience behind biblical and historic symbols with contemporary language and other phenomena that call forth similar experience. Tillich urged preachers to use contemporary language that was the functional equivalent of ancient language.

Preachers of mutual critical correlation think that the traffic should run both ways on the connectors between the ancient and contemporary worlds. Indeed, this movement is sometimes called revisionary theology because preachers are open to revising their understanding of both the tradition and the contemporary situation.[2] The preacher listens to what the text asks the congregation to believe and do and then explores the degree to which the congregation *should* regard the biblical text (or other historic Christian affirmation) as authoritative. The preacher listens to the questions in the contemporary context and gauges the degree to which they are worthwhile and appropriate questions to ask of the tradition. The preacher also listens to the ideas, values, and behaviors that contemporary people assume to be normative and questions whether we should assume them to be so. Do we need to reconsider contemporary perspectives?

Theology of Mutual Critical Correlation in Broad Outline

While most liberal preachers assume the following, virtually all preachers of mutual critical correlation do so. These points are important both as they illumine the theology of mutual correlation and as they contrast with attitudes in the evangelical community.

- Human beings wrote the Bible. The Bible contains human interpretation of God's character and purposes.

- The contents of the Bible are theologically diverse. The Bible is not a book but a library containing different theological families (for instance, priests, sages, and apocalyptists) who interpret God's purposes in different ways.

- The church needs to engage in conversation with the materials in the Bible to determine the degree to which the messages of the Bible provide guidance for today.

- The authority for the preacher engaging in mutual critical correlation is the preacher's deepest convictions concerning God. This core set of beliefs goes by other names such as the preacher's understanding of the gospel or the preacher's theological vision.

Although preachers in other theological communities sometimes speak of their interaction with the Bible as a conversation, preachers who approach the sermon through mutual critical correlation are especially prone to this idea. As in any good conversation, the text (one voice in the conversation) can raise questions that cause the preacher and congregation to reconsider their understanding of God or their faithfulness in living. At the same time, the preacher and congregation raise issues concerning the text, calling into question the adequacy of its theological vision or ethical guidance.

In this context the word *critical* does not have a negative meaning, as when the teenagers who have lived in our house explode to their parents, "Please stop being so critical of me all the time." The word *critical* functions here as it does among movie critics who evaluate a movie by identifying its strengths and weaknesses.

On the one hand, these preachers identify possible correlations between the Bible (and historic statements of faith) and today. On the other hand, such preachers evaluate the claims of particular biblical texts from the perspective of their deepest convictions about God. When these ministers find a positive correlation between what the text asks people to believe and do and the world of today, they use the text to evaluate the life of the contemporary congregation (that is, to criticize it) and to name points at which the text helps the congregation better understand God or live more faithfully. While most preachers in this tradition have great respect for the Bible and are predisposed to find a word of guidance in it for today, they argue that the Bible contains occasional ideas and images that are not only scientifically inaccurate, but also some passages that contain material that is theologically or ethically problematic.

Revisionary preachers recognize that human perception is ever changing. New discoveries sometimes render old ideas obsolete. Visiting once-discarded traditions, the preacher sometimes discovers that the old traditions provide unexpected guidance.

The ethical emphasis in mutual critical correlation is similar to themes in liberation theology. Some feminist theologians are oriented toward mutual critical correlation and others toward liberation theology. While their common goal is the liberation of women (and that of the whole human family), their methods differ slightly. Feminists of mutual critical correlation seek to construct a faith and ethic that is intelligible from the standpoint of human perception evolving on trajectories set in motion by the Enlightenment. When these feminists engage in mutual critical correlation with the tradition, the contemporary pole of the correlation is informed by a feminist urgency for equality of women and men in all arenas of life, and with keen awareness of the ongoing and multifaceted modes that males oppress women. Feminists are especially incisive in their ability to identify how the tradition blatantly and subtly reinforces male superiority in every area of life—personal relationships, the work place, economic arrangements, social freedoms. Feminists regard aspects of the tradition as authoritative when the tradition affirms egalitarianism between women and men (and calls for justice in other aspects of life), and to dismiss aspects of the tradition that discriminate between women and men. Of course, while feminism is particularly characteristic of mutual critical correlation and liberation theology, feminists are found in all the theological schools discussed in this book. We could make similar observations about the relationship between the perspectives of mutual critical correlation theology and liberation theology in regard to gay and lesbian concerns.

Similarly, some ethnic preachers operate from a framework of mutual critical correlation (rather than liberation theology). Many ethnic preachers— whether informed by ethnic theologies, liberation theology, a theology of mutual critical correlation, or a combination thereof—seek to stress God's call for a world in which all people live in equality, love, justice, dignity, freedom, and abundance.

Purposes of Preaching in the Theology of Mutual Critical Correlation

The preacher of mutual critical correlation seeks to identify possible correlations between the Bible (and historic statements of faith) while also evaluating what the particular biblical text asks the reader to believe and do from the perspective of the congregation's most reliable convictions about God. The correlation is intended to help the congregation better interpret and respond to God's purposes for individuals, the congregation, the wider community, and the world.

In the sermon in the mode of critical correlation, the preacher often helps the congregation listen to the different voices involved in the subject of the sermon, and then to assess how those voices might help (or not help) the congregation. A concern for integrity is at the heart of the revisionary approach to preaching and theology. Preachers want not to impose their own theologies on biblical texts (or other voices in the sermon) but to listen to what the biblical text invites the congregation to believe and do, and then to have a conversation regarding the degree to which the text provides adequate guidance for the congregation today.

When the congregation does not agree with the witness of a particular text, however, the sermon should move ahead to good news. It is seldom enough for a sermon to explain what a congregation does not need to believe. The revisionary sermon needs to move to a positive theological statement of how the congregation can understand and respond to the purposes of God.

Even when a biblical passage asks the congregation to believe or do something that is theologically problematic or intellectually noncredible, the act of engaging the text can be helpful. For a lively conversation sparked by a text can help the congregation clarify what it most truly believes to be true of God, and how to respond.

Preachers in the liberal tradition largely assume a hermeneutical relationship of agreement between the deeper intentions of the text and the congregation today. Preachers of mutual critical correlation sometimes distinguish between surface and deeper meanings. These latter preachers have three possible hermeneutical relationships with the text:

1. They can agree with what the text claims, in which case the purpose of the sermon is to help the congregation recognize how the text is instructive for today.

2. They can disagree with the text on theological or ethical grounds, in which case the purpose of the sermon is to explain the nature of the disagreement.

3. They can agree with some elements of the text and disagree with others, in which case the sermon needs to express appropriate affirmations and reservations.

How Preachers of Mutual Critical Correlation Might Interpret Luke 7:11-17

A preacher approaching this text through mutual critical correlation might do so in three phases. The first is to identify what the text invited people to believe from the standpoint of antiquity. This exegetical phase yields results similar to those recorded in connection with how liberals read the story of Jesus and the widow at Nain on pages 26–27. The story identifies Jesus as prophet and as agent of the realm of God, presents Jesus directly intervening in history to raise the dead person, affirms Jesus expressing God's compassion for the widow (and by extension for all marginalized people), and serves as a model for the church in Acts and for Luke's own later community.

The second phase is to compare and contrast what the text asks the congregation to believe and do with the congregation's core theological and ethical convictions. For the purpose of this illustration, I imagine a congregation whose core convictions are that God unconditionally loves each and every person and that God wills for all people to live together in love. I further assume a congregation that interprets the world in empirical terms. The idea of miracles as unilateral interventions from God in the affairs of humankind or nature is not consistent with the congregation's empirical worldview. The preacher does not believe that such things occur today, at least on a regular basis. The deeper dimensions of the text affirm God's love for the widow and for the dead person. The raising from the dead both restores the immediate relationship between the woman and the young person and provides for the woman's long-term social security.

The text does not directly run counter to the contemporary church's ethical orientation, namely that God wants people to live in love. The text does not authorize the mistreatment of people or nature. The text indirectly raises an ethical issue. If God could raise this particular person, then why did God not raise all the dead in Palestine and, indeed, in the world?

The third phase is to formulate a direction for the sermon. In this case the sermon might move on a path similar to the liberal sermon. The preacher might use a hermeneutic of analogy to help the congregation identify people and communities in situations today that are similar to that of the widow and the decedent. The essential theological move would then be to suggest how God is operating with love and compassion in those situations to bring about new life.

Questions about Mutual Critical Correlation

The same questions that I voiced about liberal theology in the preceding chapter need also to be put to theology in the mode of mutual critical correlation. Furthermore, although revisionary preachers often claim that their theological claims are confirmed by experience, the persistent practice of mutual critical correlation, while having the virtue of openness to new insight, can leave congregations wondering, "On what can we *really* count? How do we know that tomorrow the preacher might not commend some different way of thinking or acting?" The sciences, for instance, often revise their claims regarding aspects of how the world works. Things that seem certain today may seem uncertain tomorrow. Revisionary preachers need to help congregations develop critical perspectives on such processes and to realize that from age to age many in the church have adapted their understanding of Christian faith to new environments of perception.

Representative Readings

Allen, O. Wesley Jr. *Preaching Resurrection.* Preaching Classic Texts. St. Louis: Chalice, 2000. Resurrection from revisionary perspective.

———. *The Homiletic of All Believers: A Conversational Approach.* Louisville: Westminster John Knox, 2005. Preaching as part of congregational conversations over long periods of time.

Allen, Ronald J. *Believing in Preaching: The Sermon as Theological Reflection.* Louisville: Westminster John Knox, 2002. Revisionary theological method.

———. *Interpreting the Gospel: An Introduction to Preaching.* St. Louis: Chalice, 1998. Introduction to preaching from revisionary perspective.

Bond, L. Susan, *Trouble with Jesus: Women, Christology, and Preaching.* St. Louis: Chalice, 1999. Feminist, womanist, and *mujerista* themes from perspective of mutual critical correlation. Suggests "salvage" as a metaphor for preaching.

Buttrick, David. *A Captive Voice: The Liberation of Preaching.* Louisville: Westminster John Knox, 1994. Ministers preach not the content of the text but from the structure of theological meaning.

Farley, Edward. "Preaching the Bible and the Word of God," and "Toward a New Paradigm of Preaching." Idem, *Practicing Gospel: Unconventional Thoughts on the Church's Ministry.* 71–92. Louisville: Westminster John Knox, 2003. Critiques bridge paradigm. The sermon preaches not the text but core theological convictions.

Webb, Joseph M. *Preaching and the Challenge of Pluralism.* St. Louis: Chalice, 1998. Deals with diversity, collapse of certainty, increase in relativity.

———. *Old Texts, New Sermons: The Quiet Revolution in Biblical Preaching.* St. Louis: Chalice, 2000. Excellent exposition of deconstruction.

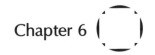

Chapter 6

Process Theology and Preaching

Process thought initially came to expression most fully through the philosophy of Alfred North Whitehead, with Charles Hartshorne being another significant exponent. A small but growing number of theologians and preachers have found that process philosophy provides concepts that help interpret Christian faith for the early twenty-first century, especially with respect to understanding God's nature and power. Process thought is also sometimes known as philosophy of organism, and theologians who make use of this way of thinking speak of *process theology* or *relational theology*. Process thought also brings forward a distinctive understanding of preaching.

Preachers in the process school often make use of mutual critical correlation, with the contemporary side of the correlation informed by a process vision of God. Process thinkers often speak in the technical vocabulary of process thought. Because that language is so different from everyday talk, I do not employ it here but describe process theology in nontechnical terms.

Process Theology in Broad Outline

The basic notion of process theology is contained in the word *process* (and its ally *becoming*) and contrasts with the focus of traditional philosophy (rooted in Greek thought) on being. Conventional philosophy seeks to describe experience by identifying the substance (or essence) of things that exist. In a gray stone, for instance, the grayness is not the essence but is an attribute that changes from stone to stone. The substance or essence is the "stone-ness" of the stone. Greek philosophy tends to understand reality as "asset of unrelated and static substances, having no internal or essential relatedness to each other."[1] For this tradition, essence is a given; the essence does not change or become but simply is. A theologian, for example, might ask, "What is the essence of the human being?"[2]

For the process theological family, reality does not consist of static entities but is constant process. Process philosophers focus not on searching for the essence of things but focus instead on becoming, that is, on how things become (or change) as a result of always relating to other things. "Always embodied (there are no unembodied selves), the self is both affected by and affects, and interacts with, a much larger social reality."[3] As Whitehead says, the "essence" of anything is, in fact, "constituted in its becoming."[4] For the process thinker, the important question is not, "What is the essential essence or substance of an entity?" but the important questions are more, "How is that entity becoming? How is that entity shaped by its relationship with other entities, and how does it shape them?"

Each moment is a fresh occasion with its own distinct possibilities and limitations. Each occasion is influenced (even if subtly) by all prior occasions, and each present occasion influences (again, sometimes subtly) all other occasions. We can see, then, why some scholars and preachers in this school like to call it relational theology—all things are inherently related to all other things so that all things affect one another.

Everything in the world is in constant process because every single thing is made up of moving parts (atoms). Each element in creation is comprised of different arrangements of atoms (for example, the wooden table on which I type, the raccoon outside, human beings). In some elements, the moving parts are arranged in more complex ways than others.

God embraces all other occasions so that all things take place in God (panentheism, as opposed to pantheism, in which God is equated to all things). Process theologians believe that God is unconditional and unsurpassable love who seeks "all inclusive well being," to use a phrase from Marjorie Suchocki.[5] From this point of view, the nature of God has two related aspects: (1) One aspect is continuity of purpose. On every occasion, God aims for all created entities to live together in love so that all experience all-inclusive well-being. That purpose is always the same. (2) God adapts the specific form of that purpose to the circumstances of each occasion. The underlying purpose is always the same—for entities to live in love—but the specific attitudes and actions that manifest love differ.

The process God has more power than any other entity, but God is not omnipotent, that is, God cannot unilaterally cause things to happen. God's power is limited. Some other theological families say that God *chooses* to limit God's use of power, but process theologians insist that God's power is limited *by nature.* The differences between God's power and all other kinds of power are twofold: God's power is utterly inexhaustible and is used always for love.

The God of process theology is omnipresent. God is always everywhere at each and every moment offering possibilities for love.

If God's power is finite, how does it work in the world? God cannot coerce people or other entities into doing things. God's power operates not by force but by lure. In each occasion, God tries to lure people toward possibilities that offer the greatest expression of love in a particular circumstance. We often experience the lure through feeling. This lure can be expressed through such things as people, nature, written texts, artworks, and possibilities for community. Within each occasion, human beings and other entities choose (either consciously or intuitively) how to respond to the lure. When people choose the highest possibility, the occasion becomes one of an optimum experience of love. When people choose lesser possibilities, then the occasion itself embodies a lesser intensity of love. However, God never rejects people or other beings but always works with each choice so God is still present to offer possibilities for love within the limitations of that choice.

Only a fraction of human awareness is conscious. Most apprehension is at the level of feeling (not just emotion but the whole gamut of awareness), a vast nonconscious realm, sometimes called the depths of experience. Although we cannot describe that realm with precision, we feel and respond to it. Other entities feel and respond to those things too, but at the level of their capacity. God is present through this realm and uses it to lure people toward inclusive well-being.

Every moment contains *some* possibility for people to experience love. Suchocki offers a practical test of whether a possibility is likely from the divine lure: when a possibility promotes all-inclusive well-being, it likely comes from God.[6]

Theologians and scholars of preaching are often attracted to process conceptuality because of how it understands God to relate to suffering and injustice. Theologians in many other families think God is completely loving, completely just, and completely powerful. Therefore, process theologians point out, God must be ultimately responsible for evil either by directly exercising divine power and *causing* evil or by refusing to use divine power to change the course of events and thereby *permitting* evil. Consequently, relational theologians argue that God cannot be simultaneously all-powerful, all-loving, and all-just. Instead, process theology believes that God is altogether loving and altogether just but is not altogether powerful. God neither causes nor permits evil, but evil results from the choices that people and other entities of creation make. Per above, however, when we make bad choices, God offers each occasion the measure of well-being possible within those choices.

Purposes of Preaching in Process Theology

The notion of proposition plays an important role in a process approach to preaching. A proposition is a lure for feeling, that is, an expression that orients people (and created beings) to certain values, practices, and interpretations of the good. The best propositions awaken people to the divine presence and purposes. A proposition may take the form of an idea (written, spoken, conceived in the brain), but it can take other forms as well (for example, art, relationships, possibilities for community).

The world is filled with propositions, some of which cohere to a greater degree with God's aim for inclusive well-being for all, others of which are much less consistent with God's purposes. A process sermon helps the congregation identify propositions that are most consistent with God's purposes and encourages the congregation to choose to cooperate with God by responding positively. The preacher also helps the congregation recognize the consequences of failing to cooperate with God. Because of sin and the relativity of human awareness, process preachers recognize that no matter how broad and deep the conversation, preachers never can fully grasp the divine lure or fully respond to it. The preacher seeks an adequate interpretation of God's presence and purposes. This conversation often takes the form of mutual critical correlation.

From this point of view, the Bible is a collection of propositions, that is, a collection of ways of understanding the divine nature and purposes and how to respond. Process theologians share the three main points regarding the Bible mentioned in the previous chapter (human authorship, contains diverse theologies, necessity of conversation with it). From the process point of view, the Bible deserves special honor because, as John B. Cobb says, "an historical emergent is best grasped in its primal form," and the Bible is a "primal form" of God's vision for the world.[7]

However, the Bible is not the only source of insight into the divine. Since God is omnipresent, people at any moment can become aware of the divine lure. One purpose of preaching is to bring different interpretations into conversation in the hope that the conversation will help clarify those that most closely embody the divine purposes.

With regard to propositions and preaching, Whitehead sets forth a striking perspective. "It is more important that a proposition be interesting than that it be true."[8] An interesting proposition stimulates thought in a way that may open the community to possibilities that it had not previously recognized.

Communities must decide which propositions are more and less adequate, but considering that contrast may help them clarify their better and worse options at a given time.

Process preachers have a vivid sense of God's relationship to preaching by seeing God active in all three phases of the sermon—in the process of preparation, in the moment of preaching itself, and in the afterglow of the sermon. God works to lure the preacher toward a mutual critical correlation that leads toward an optimum awareness and implementation of unconditional well-being. God is similarly active in the moment of preaching—with each breath, syllable, and pause, God tries to help preacher and congregation become optimally aware of the possibilities for love. Following the sermon, God is with the congregation and preacher to encourage them to respond appropriately. Yet if the sermon does not represent God's purposes adequately or if the congregation does not respond optimally, God continues to work with the choices that the preacher and congregation make to optimize the results of the choices.

How Process Preachers Might Interpret Luke 7:11-17

Process preachers would regard the story of Jesus and the widow at Nain as a proposition, a lure for feeling. As set forth in the exegesis of this story in connection with liberal theology, at the surface level the text invites people to believe that God can unilaterally intervene in the affairs of the world. At a deeper level the text invites the community to believe that God wills well-being for the widows of the world. Process preachers would likely then ponder a mutual critical correlation through conversation between this text and the world of the congregation using process categories for the contemporary side of the conversation.

Many process preachers regard the surface level of the story as not only inconsistent with our experience but, more importantly, also inconsistent with the nature of God and with the extent of divine power. The process God cannot simply arrange and rearrange events in history. However, recognizing this difference between ancient people and the process perspective, the text functions as a lure. The congregation identifies with the situation of death, and through the raising of the dead is drawn toward the possibility of greater well-being for people in similar situations today.

According to process theology God is already doing everything God can do for individuals and community in situations like that of the text. Given the importance of human responsiveness to God, the preacher could help the congregation identify concrete expressions of the divine lure toward well-being today and could recognize that the congregation's response facilitates or frustrates that movement. Most process preachers identify lure and the importance of responding in connection with circumstances such as poverty, war, hunger, exploitation, and breakdown of relationships. For example, the congregation can join with God in caring for the widows of the world and help effect well-being for the widows and for the community as a whole.

Some process preachers, however, posit the possibility of occurrences very much like the one described in the text. "Though creatures may limit the effectiveness of God's passion for wholeness, God never abandons any creature," Bruce G. Epperly notes. "Over time and in partnership with ongoing personal decision-making and a supportive community, moments of transformation may occur that would have been traditionally described as 'miraculous in nature.'" Such events "reflect a communal and personal openness to God that allows dramatic and life-changing moments to occur."[9] Dramatic transformations result from a matrix of factors coalescing divine aim, community support, personal intellectual and intuitive responsiveness, and even physiology or nature.

Questions for a Process Approach to Preaching
The biggest question faced by process preachers is the same as that faced by theologians of mutual critical correlation, namely that process preachers are in danger of remaking God in their own image. Process theology faces the additional reservation of whether its vision of a limited God is sufficient for Christian faith. One of my students refers to the God of process thought as a "wimp deity" and asks, "What is the point of believing in such a weak God?" Moreover, some critics charge not only that the leading ideas in process theology derive not from the Bible or Christian tradition but from Whitehead and Hartshorne (and not from the Bible), but also that process theology is nothing more than a convenient accommodation to modernism.

Representative Readings
Allen, Ronald J. "Preaching as Conversation among Proposals." In *Handbook of Process Theology*. Ed. Jay McDaniel and Donna Bowman, 78-90. St. Louis: Chalice, 2006. The sermon as a conversation involving different proposals.

Beardslee, William A., John B. Cobb Jr., David J. Lull, Russell Pregeant, Theodore J. Weeden Sr., and Barry A. Woodbridge. *Biblical Preaching on the Death of Jesus*. Nashville: Abingdon, 1989. Interpretation of the Passion story from a process perspective.

Suchocki, Marjorie. *The Whispered Word: A Theology of Preaching*. St. Louis: Chalice, 1999. Exquisite exposition of process approach.

Williamson, Clark M., and Ronald J. Allen. *A Credible and Timely Word: Process Theology and Preaching*. St. Louis: Chalice, 1990. Process approaches to preaching about God, injustice, hermeneutics, and biblical texts.

———. *Adventures of the Spirit: A Guide to Worship from the Perspective of Process Theology*. Lanham: University Press of America, 1997. Sermon as lure in context of a process approach.

PART THREE

Theological Movements that React against the Enlightenment

While the Enlightenment trajectory offers liberating perspectives to a large number of people, many others object to the theological directions of Enlightenment theologies. The next four chapters focus on theological movements that object to aspects of the Enlightenment agenda. Chapter 7 takes up evangelical theology. Evangelicals use Enlightenment presuppositions and methods (especially regarding truth and history) to criticize the theologies discussed in part 2.

Chapter 8 turns to neoorthodoxy, a movement that still has currency among preachers. According to Karl Barth, the church should measure its witness by its own standards and reject the notion that the church needs to measure the validity of its message against Enlightenment standards.

Postliberalism, chapter 9, takes Barth two steps farther: (1) Postliberals draw on a particular analysis of the function of language in shaping identity to intensify Barth's emphasis on the church's not measuring its witness against norms outside of itself; and (2) postliberals reject the Enlightenment idea of universal experience. For them each community's distinct language creates its own distinct experience.

Chapter 10 considers some other theologies that move away from the Enlightenment but in ways that differ from evangelicals, the neoorthodox, and postliberals. I mention confessionalism, radical orthodoxy, and theologies of otherness.

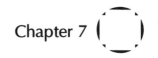
Evangelical Theology and Preaching

The term *evangelical* occurs in the church today in two ways. The older usage derives from the fact that our word *evangelical* is from the Greek word that means "good news" or "gospel." Mark 1:1, for instance, uses this word in this way: "The beginning of the *good news* [the gospel] of Jesus Christ." In the newer use the word *evangelical* refers to a specific movement in theology whose characteristics are outlined in this chapter. While I use the term in this latter way, preachers need to recognize that the evangelical theological spectrum is quite diverse. Preachers need to honor the particularities among evangelical theologies and approaches to preaching.

Evangelical Theology in Broad Outline

Evangelical theology arose in two stages: fundamentalism and then new evangelicalism. The former began in the late nineteenth century and gained force in the early twentieth century, reacting against liberal theology, especially its contention that the Bible contains material that is not historically accurate.[1] Fundamentalists argued that to provide reliable guidance, the biblical material must be historically accurate. Consequently, they reasoned, the biblical writers were under the influence of divine inspiration to record accurately events and words from the biblical period. The key theological principles for fundamentalists are as follows:

- God inspired the Bible.

- The contents of the Bible are internally self-consistent. The different materials in the Bible do not disagree with one another. Otherwise, God is inconsistent.

- The theological perspectives of the Bible are valid in every time and place. The Bible is universally true and applicable.

Using these principles preachers in this movement identified five fundamental elements of Christian theology: (1) the inerrancy of the Bible; (2) the divinity of Jesus Christ; (3) substitutionary atonement as the essential work of Christ; (4) the physical resurrection of Christ; (5) the literal, physical return of Christ. Fundamentalists sometimes engage in apologetics, that is, developing reasons to show why their perspective is believable in light of the scientific worldview.

Many early fundamentalists believed that God will condemn the larger culture, so they effectively withdrew from public life to await the return of Jesus. In the last generations—believing that God wishes for the larger culture to manifest the divine purposes—many fundamentalists have taken active roles in public life.

In the 1940s the second stage of the evangelical movement arose called the new evangelicalism. While the basic beliefs of the new evangelicals were fundamentalist in spirit, the new evangelicals were more interested in engaging contemporary social problems. Since the 1940s great diversity has developed in the evangelical movement.

While all evangelicals hold to a high doctrine of the Bible and Christian orthodoxy, evangelicals differ in how they understand God to have inspired the Bible. At one end of the inspiration spectrum (so to speak), some evangelicals think that God essentially dictated the Bible so that it is inerrant in every way, while at the other end some preachers think that human beings played a role in shaping the Bible. Thus, while virtually all evangelicals would say that "the Bible is the word of God," they differ on what they mean by that expression. Overall, however, evangelicals have more confidence in the Bible than in the power of human reason to come to a satisfactory understanding of God.

At one time, most evangelical preachers and theologians thought the Bible contains truths that should be stated in propositions. The task of the theologian and preacher, then, was to articulate the proposition that was stated or implied in every biblical text. This idea is still found in some evangelical circles. In the last generation, however, quite a few evangelicals have recognized that truth cannot always be stated in the same force or effect in a proposition as in other more imaginative forms.

Purposes of Evangelical Sermons

The primary authority in the evangelical sermon is the Bible. Indeed, J. I. Packer, a preeminent evangelical, says that preachers are to make clear that sermons are not the preacher's own ideas but are "God's message from God's book." Preachers are not to talk about the text but to allow the text to talk through them.[2]

A major purpose of the sermon is to explain the Bible and clarify its implications for today. As John Stott amplifies, the purpose of preaching is not simply to explain the Bible: "To preach is to open up the inspired text with such faithfulness and sensitivity that God's voice is heard and God's people obey."[3] However, few evangelical ministers assume that the sermon is *inherently* inspired. They reflect critically on the theological content of the sermon. Nevertheless, when the preacher is faithful to the Bible, God can work through the preacher so that the sermon is God's address to the congregation:

> God speaks through the Bible. It is the major tool of communication by which [God] addresses individuals today. Biblical preaching, therefore, must not be equated with the 'old, old story of Jesus and his love,' as though it were retelling history about better times when God was alive and well. Nor is preaching merely a rehash of ideas about God—traditional, but removed from life. Through the preaching of the Scriptures, God encounters men and women to bring them to salvation (2 Tim. 3:15) and to richness and ripeness of Christian character (2 Tim. 3:16-17).[4]

When the evangelical preacher reaches clarity regarding what the ancient text asks the listeners to believe and do, the preacher has grasped what the text continues to ask the contemporary congregation to believe and do. Hermeneutics is determining how to apply the ancient Bible in and for the present.

Among fundamentalists and evangelicals, sermons have two widely accepted purposes. The first is conversion of sinners while the second is building up the body of Christ for witness. In some evangelical circles, the service of worship climaxes with an invitation for unconverted people to make a confession of faith. In many evangelical bodies, however, the overtly evangelistic quality of the sermon in the service has diminished, with the typical sermon now aiming to help the congregation grow in faith.

Some preachers in these movements also see a third related purpose for preaching, namely helping the members of the congregation recognize how to express their convictions in public life (for instance, through taking certain positions on social issues, working for certain kinds of legislation and social programs, and even voting in civic elections for particular candidates).

An evangelical sermon usually centers in the exposition of a passage from the Bible. The preacher explains the significance of the passage for today while sometimes drawing on other parts of the Bible. This approach depends on the Bible being internally self-consistent. Many evangelical sermons have a teaching quality. Some evangelicals, though, do preach sermons that deal with more than one passage, indeed linking together many different biblical verses and passages.

How Evangelicals Might Interpret Luke 7:11-17

Given evangelical diversity we cannot report *the* evangelical interpretation of this text. We can, however, identify some themes that could appear in evangelical sermons. Some preachers identify the propositions the preacher can draw from this story. However, some evangelicals think revelation can be expressed in forms other than propositions.

Evangelical preachers tend to take the story as a factual report of an encounter that took place in Nain. Occasionally evangelical ministers might turn to apologetics to demonstrate the likelihood, from a scientific or philosophical perspective, that miracles such as this one occurred in the past and can occur today. Evangelical preachers might see Jesus' ability to perform supernatural miracles as demonstrating that Jesus is the Son of God. They might also call attention to the raising from the dead as part of Jesus' announcement of the apocalyptic coming of the realm of God. The fact that a miracle occurred contributes to confidence in the return of Jesus as an apocalyptic event.

Some evangelical leaders might use the story of Jesus raising the widow's child as a model for what the congregation today can expect from God. Just as God intervened in the desperate circumstances of the widow, so the congregation can turn to God for direct intervention today. The preacher would want to explain the circumstances in which the congregation might expect such interventions. What does the congregation count on? What does the congregation need to do, especially in the way of demonstrating faith? Given the fact that God does not always appear to act in ways that congregants expect or ask, the preacher should also offer an explanation of why such miracles may not occur. Some evangelicals believe that the age of miracles ceased at the end of the apostolic period. Such preachers need to explain why God stopped performing miracles.

Some evangelicals see the story as a call to ministries today that are analogous to Jesus' caring for the widow. Such evangelicals would see the statement that Jesus had compassion for the widow as a model for their own compassion for people today who are in situations similar to the widow.

An increasing number of evangelical preachers would seek to identify how and why this particular story represents the biblical and theological method of the entire Gospel of Luke. They would presume the event itself as true but look beyond the event to Luke's theological message for his readers.

Questions for Evangelical Preaching

Many preachers who think that the Bible contains different theological viewpoints challenge the evangelical emphasis upon the Bible as internally self-consistent. More substantially, evangelical preachers maintain, with many other Christians, that God is altogether loving, altogether powerful, and altogether just. Undeserved suffering tests this conviction. Preachers from the process family object that if God is altogether powerful, then God could intervene in history at any moment to end undeserved suffering. If God has the power to do so, but does not act, then God is not altogether loving or just. Evangelicals also face the question of how to deal with biblical texts that are theologically and ethically troubling, exemplified in Psalm 137:9: "Happy shall they be who take your little ones and dash them against the rock!" Would a God of love inspire such a horrific act? Some evangelicals ask congregations to suspend what they usually assume to be true of the world, especially aspects of the scientific worldview. To many people, occurrences such as Jesus raising the child in Nain do not appear to be a pattern that people today can count on. When interventions do not appear to occur in the way a preacher says, the congregation wonders what they can count on from God.

Representative Readings

Adam, Peter. *Speaking God's Words: A Practical Theology of Preaching.* Leicester: InterVarsity, 1996. An evangelical theology of preaching.

Chappel, Bryan. *Christ-Centered Preaching: Redeeming the Expository Sermon.* Grand Rapids: Baker, 1994. Pervasive focus on Christ as center of preaching.

Greidanus, Sidney. *The Modern Preacher and the Ancient Text: Interpreting and Preaching Biblical Literature.* Grand Rapids: Eerdmans, 1988. Literary and rhetorical criticism through an evangelical lens.

Larsen, David L. *The Anatomy of Preaching: Identifying the Issues in Preaching Today.* Grand Rapids: Kregel, 1999. Authority and other important issues.

Logan, Samuel T. Jr., ed. *The Preacher and Preaching: Reviving the Art in the Twentieth Century.* Phillipsburg: Presbyterian and Reformed, 1986. Eighteen scholars explain all aspects of preaching from an evangelical point of view.

Robinson, Haddon W. *Biblical Preaching: The Development and Delivery of Expository Messages.* Grand Rapids: Baker, 1980. Classic evangelical discussion.

Stott, John R. W. *Between Two Worlds: The Art of Preaching in the Twentieth Century.* Grand Rapids: Eerdmans, 1982. Widely respected statement.

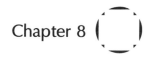

Chapter 8

Neoorthodox Theology and Preaching

Many preachers embraced neoorthodoxy (also known as dialectical theology or crisis theology) in the middle years of the twentieth century. Its progenitors include Karl Barth, Emil Brunner, and Reinhold Niebuhr. While the neoorthodox theologians were diverse, the movement as a whole believed that preaching is key for people to encounter the Word of God. Barth envisioned his massive *Church Dogmatics* as serving preaching.[1] Some preachers continue to operate with neoorthodox assumptions. Barth's theology is midwife to postliberalism (chap. 9). I now offer some general characterizations of neoorthodoxy but concentrate on the theology of Karl Barth because his approach still informs a fair number of preachers.

Neoorthodox Theology in Broad Outline

The first generation of neoorthodox theologians reacted against Schleiermacher and liberalism because of two factors. One was the horror of the First World War, which repudiated the liberal assumption that the world was progressively getting better. Barth was distressed that many German liberal theologians supported the war. The other factor was pastoral experience. In serving a church, Barth noticed that worshipers expected a word from God whereas his training had prepared him to talk only about human feelings and interpretations. Barth concluded that liberal forays outside Christian sources inevitably prompt Christians to make idols of cultural realities. In this context the neoorthodox theologians sought to reclaim Reformation sensibilities. (Note that neoorthodoxy differs from radical orthodoxy, discussed in chapter 10.)

The neoorthodox theologians developed the alternative claim that human beings can learn about God's character and purposes only from divine revelation. Expanding on Søren Kierkegaard, the early phase of neoorthodoxy regarded God as wholly other. Because God is a being of infinite qualitative distinction from humankind, whatever we can know of God must come from God's own revelation. Later neoorthodox reflection would soften the edges of the distinction somewhat between God and humankind such that even Barth would write about the humanity of God.[2] However, neoorthodox theology always stressed that when God's Word confronts human beings, it creates a crisis for us (hence the name *crisis theology*): Will we understand ourselves in terms of God's revelation, or will we understand ourselves in terms of our idolatry and rebellion?

What is the source of divine revelation? The key answer is: the Word of God. Barth articulated an understanding of the Word that many preachers continue to follow today. The Word of God takes three forms: the incarnate Word (Jesus Christ), the written Word (the Bible), and the preached Word (the sermon). These three forms express the same Word that God definitively manifest in Jesus Christ. For Barth and for many preachers influenced by neoorthodoxy, the incarnate Christ *is* the Word (though the Word can be expressed in three forms). While Barth thought that we can know God *only* through Jesus Christ, Emil Brunner believed that humankind could learn something of God through natural theology. Barth replied in a pamphlet titled simply *Nein!* ("No!").[3]

For Barth, the truth of Christian faith does not depend upon criteria external to the Christian community such as the exercise of human reason or the discoveries of the sciences. The truth of Christian faith is self-authenticating. The Word itself provides the only norm whereby its expressions can be judged. When explicating Christian doctrine Barth draws largely from the Bible with occasional reference to historic creeds that voice orthodox Christian thinking as well as from traditional Christian theologians (such as Anselm). According to Barth, the church can interpret its own life only from within its own sources or face the possibility of remaking its faith in terms of the world.

The purpose of the church is to testify to God's revelation; a great danger the church faces is becoming self-preoccupied and thinking of its life as an end in itself. When that happens, the church becomes its own idol and God must speak the Word afresh to it. The church cannot allow the culture to shape the church's thinking but must speak the Word in and to the culture so that the culture has the opportunity to conform itself to the values of the Word. Otherwise, the culture is condemned.

Purposes of Sermons in Neoorthodox Theology

The Bible is central in neoorthodox preaching. Barth's attitude toward the Bible is crucial but is difficult to describe. On the one hand, Barth accepted critical biblical interpretation that attempted to locate biblical texts in their ancient historical and literary contexts. Barth did not regard the Bible as inspired in the same way as evangelicals (chap. 7). On the other hand, the congregation can encounter the Word when it gathers around the Bible. The words of the Bible remain human words, but when God touches them, they *become* words through which God speaks. The Bible is not the Word of God, nor does the Bible contain the Word. Rather, the Bible becomes the occasion of the Word of God when God graciously speaks a living address to the congregation through Jesus Christ as the congregation gathers around the Bible.

In a way that elevates preaching to a position unequalled in almost any other contemporary theological family, Barth regards preaching as one of the three forms of the Word of God. Jesus Christ commissions preaching, which Barth defines as "the attempt, essayed by one called thereto in the church, to express in [that person's] own words in the form of an exposition of a portion of the biblical testimony to revelation, and to make comprehensible to [people of the preacher's] day, the promise of God's revelation, reconciliation, and calling, as they are to be expected here and now."[4]

Barth thus has a very lively understanding of God's relationship to the sermon. For Barth, the human words of the preacher can become the Word of God *when* God graciously makes them so. Every sermon does not *necessarily* become the Word of God but does so when the preacher is faithful to the Bible and when God moves in the moment of preaching to make the sermon the Word. The sermon is a set of human words that can become a message "in which and through which God . . . speaks about [Godself]."[5] The sermon as Word of God thus puts before the congregation the crisis of making a choice of either accepting or rejecting the Word. From this perspective the preacher is a herald through whom God speaks to the congregation.

The neoorthodox preacher is in a peculiar position. On the one hand, the preacher is called to prepare a sermon, although Barth discourages the preacher from becoming entranced with the form or content of the sermon. Creativity too easily can become an end in itself, calling attention to the preacher and distracting the congregation from the Word. The most important aspects of sermon preparation are to nurture a receptive attitude to the biblical text so that the sermon can "cause the testimony present in the text to be heard." The preacher is to "bring to life in his present age the testimony of the prophets and the apostles."[6] On the other hand, the sermon does not become the Word of God unless God makes it so. The effectiveness of the sermon—whether it becomes the Word of God—does not depend upon the preacher's creativity or even on the preacher's pastoral analysis of the congregation but only on the movement of God.

How Neoorthodox Preachers Might Interpret Luke 7:11-17

In a sense it is beside the point to ask how the neoorthodox *preacher* might *interpret* this text since *God* will use this text in the sermon as an occasion to address the congregation with God's own word. However, Barth's comments about this text in his *Church Dogmatics* point to the themes that rose to the level of importance as Barth attended to this text in the manner described at the end of the preceding discussion.

Barth is drawn to the figure of Jesus Christ in the text as the incarnate Word of God. Through Jesus, God confronts the situation in Nain when the "alien will and unknown power invaded the general course of things" and actualized an aspect of the realm of God in the very presence of the people. "The customary order was breached by an incursion the possibility of which they could not explain."[7] Noting that translations such as "to have mercy" or "to have pity" or "to have compassion" are inadequate to describe Jesus' response to the situation of the widow and the child (and others as well), Barth says, poignantly, that the situation "went right into [Jesus'] heart . . . so that their whole plight was now His own, and as such He saw and suffered it far more keenly than they did." Jesus "took their misery upon Himself, taking it away from them and making it His own."[8]

Drawing a parallel between this text and the story of the raising of Jairus's daughter, Barth also sees the text pointing to God's intention to "work against the rule of death in the cosmos." Indeed, "Death was something which they [the people in antiquity] all thought it a self-evident law of reason and custom to regard as an unassailable fact, and therefore to treat with pious sentimentality as a supreme power." Jesus, however, "denied both the law and the power." In a gripping statement, Barth says, "When [Jesus] enters this house, it can no longer be a house of death."[9]

The story demonstrates the fact that God's ways are hidden from us. For, like other stories of raisings of the dead in the New Testament, it does not "fully narrate and describe" the event.[10]

The text describes Jesus as a prophet, indicating that Jesus is certainly a source of the knowledge of God.[11] The witnesses are "on the right track" when they give glory to God because they recognize that Jesus is a great prophet.[12] However, Barth chides the people in Nain who acclaim Jesus a "great prophet" for not recognizing that Jesus is much more than a prophet.[13]

Questions for Neoorthodoxy

Neoorthodox preachers seem to assume that the Word of God can address us in an almost pure, direct state. However, all human expression and even all human awareness is interpretive. To what degree does the Word of God indeed create its own hearing and to what degree is every perception of that Word compromised by the inherent interpretive aspects of human awareness? Neoorthodox theologians do not always consider the possibility that their understanding of the Word of God might be idolatrous. Indeed, in neoorthodox preaching, it is sometimes difficult to hear how the Word specifically addresses the congregation in its particular context. How can we distinguish *the* Word from words that may be inadequate? When it comes to the Bible, neoorthodox preachers sometimes read their later theological assumptions into texts. This eisegetical tendency is especially true with respect to interpreting the First Testament through the lens of Jesus Christ, though Barth is among the most respectful theologians of his generation with regard to Judaism. Occasional neoorthodox preachers *assume* their sermons *are* the Word of God in such a way as to make their sermons idols, and to do so with arrogance that destroys community.

Representative Readings

Achtemeier, Elizabeth. *Preaching from the Old Testament.* Louisville: Westminster John Knox, 1989. One of many books with a neoorthodox spin written by Achtemeier.

Bartow, Charles L. *God's Human Speech: A Practical Theology of Proclamation.* Grand Rapids: Eerdmans, 1997. Neoorthodox approach to preaching in context of performance theory.

Farris, Stephen. *Preaching That Matters: The Bible and Our Lives.* Louisville: Westminster John Knox, 1999. A hermeneutic of analogy powered to help congregations encounter God's Word for today.

Ritschl, Dietrich. *A Theology of Proclamation.* Richmond: John Knox, 1963. Barthian approach with practical suggestions for developing sermons.

Willimon, William H. *Conversations with Barth on Preaching.* Nashville: Abingdon, 2006. Post-liberal interpretation of Barth's leading themes. Illustrated with Barth's sermons.

Wilson, Paul Scott. *God Sense: Reading the Bible for Preaching.* Nashville: Abingdon, 2001. Recovery of ancient approaches to hearing God's Word through text.

———. *The Four Pages of the Sermon: A Guide to Biblical Preaching* Nashville: Abingdon, 1999. Envisions sermon as four pages through which congregation can encounter God's Word.

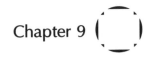

Chapter 9

Postliberal Theology and Preaching

As the name *"postliberal"* suggests, postliberals also seek to transcend liberalism. Indeed, this movement objects to the liberal spirit in theology and preaching, and its followers see the church as a countercultural community that models an alternative set of values and practices to those of the larger world. However, whereas evangelicals use modern views of science, truth, and history to undercut liberalism, postliberal preachers bypass these concerns and turn to a distinct understanding of the relationship of language and social experience. Postliberals build on some of Barth's emphases but reframe others.

Postliberal Theology in Broad Outline

Postliberal preachers share with Barth the conviction that the church needs to maintain its own distinct identity so that it can offer God's alternative way of thinking and acting to the idolatrous larger world. Hans Frei joins Barth in saying that the significance of a biblical text should not be measured by the scientific (modern, Enlightenment) worldview, for that means that the content of Christian faith is accountable to a standard of reference outside the Bible.[1] The biblical materials are realistic (lifelike) even if they cannot be empirically verified. Instead, Frei urges the preacher (and theologian) to *begin with the Bible and other traditional Christian texts* as containing the normative stories that form the identity of the Christian community.

Postliberals further ground this way of thinking in a distinctive understanding of how language and practice function to form identity. Liberals talk and act on the basis of deep feeling. Contrariwise, postliberals see language and community practices *forming* (not expressing) interior life and behavior. As George Lindbeck puts it, to be religious is to "interiorize a set of skills" that are "communicated through the language of the community and through what people do."[2]

Postliberal thinkers read the Bible as a more-or-less continuous narrative of God's relationship to the world. Preachers in the postliberal school tend to see traditional Christian doctrine after the Bible as providing grammar that helps the congregation regulate faith. Postliberal preachers are often christocentric, regarding Jesus Christ as the climax of the biblical story and as the normative center of the language and practice of the church.

Postliberal preachers eschew the efforts of liberals to correlate biblical values with contemporary notions in an effort to help people with Enlightenment or post-Enlightenment mentalities accept the gospel. Postliberal preachers fear that such liberal efforts too easily can compromise Christian identity and message.

The term *practice* refers to things the community does that embody important community values, such as prayer, participation in the bread and the cup, studying the Bible together, seeking justice for the poor, and calling for peace in the world. By doing such things repeatedly, these behaviors move from being external demonstrations to becoming expressions of the most ingrained values of individuals and communities.

The distinctive language and practices of the church create the church as a distinctive culture. For North American congregations, the church witnesses to God's values in the midst of the larger culture of consumerism and imperialism, idolatry, injustice, exploitation, and violence. The postliberal church is countercultural. As William Willimon and Stanley Hauerwas say, the church is a colony of "resident aliens."[3]

Ministers in the postliberal tradition emphasize that preachers should build up the congregation as community. For community is fundamental to the formation of the Christian self (which is, by postliberal definition, a self always in community) and is the instrument whereby Christian witness takes place in the world.

The biblical narrative is the primary authority in postliberal sermons. Preachers commend ideas and events that are consistent with the biblical story while they critique aspects of life that are inconsistent with that story. Postliberal preachers do not use materials from the sciences or philosophy to posit the credibility of Christian faith. As Hauerwas and Willimon put it, the preacher's task "is not to make the gospel credible to the modern world, *but to make the world credible to the gospel.*"[4]

Postliberal preachers speak of the Word of God as Jesus Christ, but whereas Barth believes that God becomes *present* in Jesus Christ, many postliberals are reticent to speak of Christ as *present*. Charles L. Campbell notices that Frei "directs preaching beyond individual, experiential events to the building up of the church as a people who embody and witness to Jesus Christ's *indirect* *'presence'* and thereby God's reign in the world."[5] Christ is not directly present in the church or the world. The preaching of the church, the church's identity-shaping practices, and the church's enacting its identity in social settings beyond the church are the *means* whereby Christ is known—and effectively present. "The church is now the spatial and temporal basis of the presence of Jesus in the world. The church, that is, embodies Jesus' indirect presence in and for the world."[6]

Purposes of Postliberal Sermons

In the postliberal community preaching is "a practice of constituting a people."[7] The sermon speaks not to individuals about their problems and possibilities nor about social issues but builds up the congregation as community in the identity of Jesus Christ so the congregation can enact that identity. Preaching is a practice whose goal is to form the congregation into a community that embodies Jesus Christ.[8]

The preacher goes about this task by narrating the congregation into the biblical world. The preacher uses and clarifies the specific language and grammar of the Bible (and Christian doctrine) and does not try to find contemporary equivalents for biblical concepts. Indeed, as Richard Lischer says, the preacher's most basic task is to teach the church how to talk.[9] Preaching also helps the congregation learn the practices that are essential to Christian identity.

Preaching in the postliberal movement further guides the congregation in how to enact its identity through witness in the larger social world. Preachers in this movement do not simply comment on social issues, nor do they simply point out how to interpret issues from the perspective of political correctness. Postliberal sermons call the congregation's attention to what Christian identity requires in the way of attitude and behavior in the face of particular social situations. The sermon is particularly aimed at helping the congregation distinguish between popular (but degenerate) assumptions and Christian interpretation and action. For example, according to many postliberals, nonviolence is constitutive of Christian identity. The congregation, then, must resist war, capital punishment, and other uses of violence.

How Postliberals Might Interpret Luke 7:11-17

Both revisionary and evangelical preachers are interested in whether Jesus actually raised the dead person as told in the story in Luke 7:11-17. Postliberals do not share this interest. They are content to regard this story as a realistic narrative. The postliberal interest is in how this story helps the congregation redescribe its perception of the world in view of Jesus Christ as narrated in the specific circumstances of this text.[10]

Indeed, for many postliberal preachers the primary focus of the sermon will be on the figure of Jesus Christ. Many postliberals would say that Jesus Christ in this text embodies God's realm whereas the woman and the deceased person represent qualities of life that defy that realm. Jesus Christ relates to the widow and the decedent with the same compassion that God shows toward Israel, thus signaling that Jesus seeks to relate similarly to all systems of marginalization, insecurity, and death (whether literally or by virtue of circumstances that are living death).

A sermon might seek to make Jesus Christ indirectly present for the congregation in the way that Jesus is narrated in this short biblical passage. Through the language of the sermon, the preacher might aim for the congregation to encounter Jesus Christ, embodiment of the divine realm, as indirectly manifest in the sermon itself. Given the fact that postliberal preachers envision Jesus Christ as present through the church as community, the preacher might want to alert the congregation to how they encounter Jesus Christ demonstrating compassion in the community of the church and beyond.

A postliberal preacher might redescribe the world as a domain in which death is not the ultimate power. According to this text, people can live in freedom from power and threat of death for the event of Jesus Christ redescibes the world and its possibilities.[11]

With respect to the congregation's enacting its identity as community of Jesus Christ beyond its own life, the preacher may want to help the congregation consider how the congregation as community can embody the divine realm in the world today in ways that are consistent with how Jesus is pictured in this text. Where and how can the congregation enact compassion similar to that of Jesus in relationship with the marginalized, insecure, and dead in the contemporary setting?

Questions for Postliberal Preaching

Postliberals repeatedly speak of *the* biblical story and of Christian faith in the singular without acknowledging diverse theologies in the Bible. This is especially problematic when speaking of *the* story of Jesus as the center of the biblical story. Which story of Jesus is considered *the* story—Mark, Matthew,

Luke, John, or Paul? By interpreting the Bible through the lenses of the historic (but postbiblical) affirmations of faith, postliberals sometimes read later doctrine into the earlier biblical witness. By refusing to measure the reliability of Christian witness against norms outside the Bible and Christian claims, some preachers think that postliberals engage in circular reasoning. Many people want to know *why* they should believe that a certain interpretation of Christian faith is reliable other than the fact that the Bible says so.

Representative Readings

Campbell, Charles L. *Preaching Jesus: New Directions for Homiletics in Hans Frei's Postliberal Theology*. Grand Rapids: Eerdmans, 1997. The most thorough exposition of postliberal approach to preaching.

——. *The Word Before the Powers: An Ethic of Preaching*. Louisville: Westminster John Knox, 2002. A contemporary classic.

Eslinger, Richard L. *Narrative Imagination: Preaching the Worlds that Shape Us*. Nashville: Abingdon, 1995. A postliberal approach in dialogue with David Buttrick's approach to the sermon.

Green, Joel B., and Michael Pasquarello. *Narrative Reading, Narrative Preaching: Reuniting New Testament Interpretation and Proclamation*. Grand Rapids: Baker Academic, 2003. Interpretations of Gospels and Acts, Letters, Apocalypse).

Lischer, Richard. "Preaching as the Church's Language." In *Listening to the Word: Studies in Honor of Fred B. Craddock*. Ed. Gail R. O'Day and Thomas G. Long, 113–30. Nashville: Abingdon, 1993. Preaching moving from event to formation, from illustration to narrative, and from translation to performance.

Shepherd, William H. *No Deed Greater than a Word: A New Approach to Biblical Preaching*. Lima: CSS, 1998. Postliberal sermon preparation.

Willimon, William H. *Peculiar Speech: Preaching to the Baptized*. Grand Rapids: Eerdmans, 1992. Willimon is the most prolific postliberal author. This title is representative of his fifty-plus books.

Chapter 10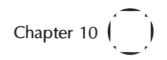

Other Theologies and Preaching
Confessional Theology, Radical Orthodoxy, and Theologies of Otherness

The title "Other Theologies" is a double entendre. At one level, it straight-forwardly refers to three theological houses not previously mentioned that have reservations about Enlightenment values. At another level, the designa-tion "Other Theologies" also echoes one of the theological families discussed here—theologies that assume otherness as one of their formative categories. In different ways each of these families is uncomfortable with the modern quests for certainty and for principles that are universally valid. I discuss three such theological houses—confessional theology, radical orthodoxy, and the-ologies of otherness.

Other Theologies in Very Broad Outline

Confessional theology seeks a middle way between liberal and postliberal theological visions. The confessional theologians agree that the modern goal of absolute and universal certainty is not achievable. Yet this preacher also believes that the postmodern emphases on the relativity and particularity of all awareness leaves the believer on the edge of chaos. Between these two poles, David Lose, the preeminent scholar of confessional preaching, seeks "critical fideism, that, while it cannot prove the truth of its ultimate claims [via modern-scientific-philosophical criteria], nevertheless seeks to make a case in the public arena for their utility and soundness."[1] By having a public discussion of criteria and truthfulness, confessionalists aim to avoid the insularity and circularity of postliberalism as well as the liberal tendency toward universal certainty. Through a "pragmatic assessment of our ordinary practices," these preachers hope to provide "some form of foundationalism," that is, something people believe.[2] The congregation operates as if the claims of Christian faith are true. Although the confessions cannot be proven in a conventional sense, the congregation believes them because when we participate in them, the congregation's faith is kindled or rekindled.

The term *confession* is clearly defined and is distinct from the notion of personal testimony that is popular in many congregations today. Following the lead of the Second Testament, confession includes (1) essential elements of Christian tradition and (2) "articulation and actualization of that tradition in response to the church's proclamation and its present circumstances."[3] The minister helps the church rediscover the practical implications of its core confessions, both formal (such as the Nicene affirmation of faith) and informal (what folk in the barbershop believe). The church does not regard the confessions as "tests of orthodoxy" but as "instruments to 'nurture and engender faith.'"[4]

For confessional theologians the irreducible Christian confession is Jesus Christ as the definitive manifestation of God's purposes. While confession starts in the witness to the resurrection of Christ, confessionalism sees this Word only in the context of the many and various ways that God spoke in the First Testament. While confessional theology regards the revelation in Christ as the clearest self-revelation of the God of Israel, confessionalists do not regard the revelation in Christ as God's only Word.

Radical orthodoxy objects to the split between the secular and the sacred that came about as a result of the Enlightenment. They object further to modernity's propensity to set aside tradition and to regard individualism as a crowning value. Radical orthodox preachers seek to interpret the whole of life in theological perspective, in a way reminiscent of the premodern vision of life as a religious whole whose various parts are interconnected.

Radical orthodoxy criticizes the secularism of contemporary Western culture. "Speaking with a microphoned and digitally simulated voice, [secularism] proclaims—uneasily or else increasingly unashamedly—its own lack of values and lack of meaning." Moreover, "In its cyberspaces and theme-parks, [secularism] promotes a materialism which is soulless, aggressive, nonchalant, and nihilistic."[5] Theologians in this camp believe that such emptiness is characteristic of every aspect of contemporary life and that it results from the fact that, under the influence of the Enlightenment, theology has been divorced from every other enterprise and has become little more than a source of personal renewal for people who are weary from too many hours on meaningless jobs, too much meaningless shopping, and trying to fill the void of meaning in other meaningless ways. Academic disciplines (such as the social sciences) and other arenas of human endeavor aggravate this problem by not situating their "concerns and activities in a theological framework."[6] Modern theology itself contributes to this situation by turning to secular disciplines for norms. The radically orthodox criticize (1) theologies of correlation as compromised by excessive reliance on secular authorities and (2) neoorthodox theologies as adhering to a false dichotomy between revelation and reason.

The name of this movement, radical orthodoxy, suggests the way forward.[7] The movement is radical in the etymological sense of that term—returning to the roots or origins. The movement is orthodox in that the roots to which it returns are "creedal Christianity and the exemplarity of its patristic mix"—as interpreted by radical orthodoxy—especially Christology, the Trinity, the church, and the Eucharist.[8] Where other schools of theology "can tend to the ploddingly exegetical, radical orthodoxy mingles exegesis, cultural reflection and philosophy in a complex but coherently executed *collage*."[9]

The writers of radical orthodoxy believe that all things derive from God. God invites human beings to participate in the divine life. The Trinity reveals that reality is, at its heart, participatory. An important notion is participation, for participation in the divine life is the only antidote to secularism and impersonal chaos. The world is caught up in God and the incarnation shows that God is immanently and ever in the world. The Eucharist sensitizes us to participating in the larger world. As Charles W. Allen notes, "As bread is broken, we find we have been participating all along in that shape . . . and now we are drawn to an unendingly fuller, more wholesome participation that leads us well beyond the parish walls. This, we can't help believing, is the desired shape of all life everywhere."[10] Participation in the church is not an end but is a means to help the community discover how to participate more fully in God in every aspect of life. God aims for all elements of creation to live together in mutually supportive harmony.

For *theologies of otherness,* the category of the other (difference, alterity, or strange-ness/er) is formative. These theologies object to the Enlightenment emphasis on universal experience. They conclude that the Enlightenment quest for universal experience has led westerners not to respect the particular experiences and values of people of other cultures. Indeed, Eurocentric westerners often seek to suppress difference and want other people to be like them. For years, for instance, the United States described itself as a melting pot in which people were to give up the particularities of their cultures of origin.

Theologians of otherness note that each person, each community, each culture, indeed each element of creation is a distinct entity with its own identity and particularity. Emmanuel Lévinas, a leading inspiration in otherness, contrasts respect for others with the urge toward sameness (or the infinity of particularity in contrast with the totalizing of universality).[11] When we perceive others only in terms of ourselves, we not only misperceive but also do violence to them. Theologies of otherness insist on respecting the particularity of others—individuals, communities, cultures, and elements of nature. By honoring such distinctiveness, we allow the richness of difference and diversity to permeate and shape the world more and, therefore, to enrich our own lives.

Preachers in this theological house further view the encounter with the other as an opportunity to discover things about ourselves that we may not recognize and that we may want to reinforce or to change. Becoming aware of others pushes us to name our assumptions and to think critically about them. The presence of the other may open us to possibilities for life that we have not previously identified. By attending to the other we may discover that we have more in common than we expected. Appreciation of the other should cause one to lose arrogance and to approach others with a deep sense of humility.

Theologies of otherness regard one of God's fundamental purposes as seeking a world in which all others (and oneself) can live in ways that honor the integrity of each. God seeks a world of respectful relationships facilitating encounters that generate support for others. Of course, individuals and communities must resist the activities of those who seek to exploit, abuse, or otherwise violate the integrity of others. We never can fully know others, but we can assert their value and help shape the world as a safe space for them and for continuing encounters.

Purposes of Preaching in These Other Theologies

David Lose succinctly states the purpose of preaching in *confessional theology:* "that the hearer may believe the Word proclaimed, enter into the identity offered, and articulate and thereby actualize the tradition for him or herself (appropriation) through the power of the Holy Spirit."[12] The sermon "is a provisional monologue that seeks but does not coerce, a response of faith from those who hear."[13] The sermon has a narrative-kerygmatic quality in that the preacher is to take the narrative confessions of Scripture and articulate the central promise of the text and invite the congregation to make sense of their lives in terms of the narrative and the promises of the gospel.[14] Such preaching involves, simultaneously, critical distance from Christian tradition and critical participation in it.[15] The preacher's role is to "offer her confession of the meaning and import of the [biblical] text to the gathered assembly in a way that both grounds hearers in a narrative, communal identity while simultaneously safeguarding the space in which they can appropriate, rather than merely give their assent to, the gospel proclaimed."[16]

To this point theologians of *radical orthodoxy* have given little direct atten-tion to preaching. Rowan Williams, Archbishop of Canterbury, while not fully identified with radical orthodoxy but sometimes cited as a kindred spirit, offers a perspective on preaching that is consistent with the values of radical orthodoxy. The sermon is part of the "Eucharistic transaction." As Williams says, "We are there at the Eucharist so that we may be changed into [the like-ness of Jesus Christ], from glory to glory. We are not there to change certain things in the world, which we then adore from a distance. We are there so that the transubstantiation may occur *in us*."[17] Preaching itself has a sacramental quality in radical orthodoxy because its subject matter is transformation. The very act of talking about such transformation is itself a part of the transfor-mational event.

Williams turns to Dietrich Bonhoeffer to "compare preaching to the holding out of a large red apple to a hungry child."[18] Because secularism so penetrates perception, the preacher may need to help the congregation recognize its hunger and point to participation in the divine as the way to satisfaction. For the Archbishop, preaching "is transformed speech because it does not just repeat what the world says, nor does it just repeat what the Bible says. It attempts to show, in its movement, in its direction and imagery, what it is to be in a different world, another [dominion]. It is an invitation to the [Dominion] of God."[19] This new world is already present because all things are already in God.

Preachers may give an exposition of the Bible, but exposition is not the heart of the sermon. The preacher uses the Bible as a part of "saying that a change has occurred. You think through the changes, the transformations in the Scriptures, as you proclaim, because what you are proclaiming is an act of transformation."[20] The purpose of the sermon is not to preach the text but is to preach transformation.

To speak of *the* purpose of preaching in *theologies of otherness* would be to betray one of the fundamental values of those theologies by stating the purpose of preaching in terms of sameness, totalizing, or universality. How-ever, a formative scholar of otherness in preaching, John S. McClure, makes a dramatic statement in this regard:

> The beginning of other-wise preaching is in other-wise *commitment*: commitment to human others of all shapes and sizes and a personal and theological commitment to exiting the biblical, theological, social, experiential, and cultural hegemonies that exist within and beyond the churches. No matter what form it takes, other-wise commit-ment feels deeply the proximity of human others and the nearness of an impinging alternative reign of God in which things are indeed other-wise. This commitment is

more than an outward display of solidarity, as important as that can be. It involves decisive, existential caring. Lévinas makes it clear that fullness of life is found only in our openness to the absolute mystery of the other. In the neighbor's face (*visage*), we experience an absolute obligation towards compassion, resistance, justice, and hope that grips our lives and holds us to a new vision for all humanity.[21]

The preacher of otherness is to bring others together for a face-to-face encounter that allows each party to encounter the others that are part of the moment of preaching in such a way as to want to move toward commitment and caring.

The task of the preacher of otherness is, thus, often twofold: (1) The preacher needs to help the congregation resist the urge toward sameness with respect to others in the realm of the sermon. That is, preachers need to encourage the congregation not to view others as projections of their own images. To accomplish this task the preacher may need to help the congregation deconstruct their preexisting (or embedded or naive) perceptions of others involved in the interaction. (2) The preacher is called to help the congregation recognize the possibilities for understanding and behavior that are raised by the presence of the others. In order to carry out these tasks, preachers themselves need always to reflect critically on their own tendencies toward sameness and to be willing to deconstruct and reconceive their self-interpretations and their interpretations of others.

Others involved in preaching include God, the Bible, the congregation (and the larger church), and others beyond the congregation and the church. God is the great Other. The preacher needs particularly to help the congregation avoid idolatry (that is, not honoring the otherness of God). The preacher also needs to be self-critical of the preacher's own tendency to make idols of the preacher's own perceptions of God. The Bible is a library of others. The purpose of biblical exegesis, from this point of view, is to allow the preacher and the congregation to perceive the otherness of the text so that the encounter with the text can open the congregation to fresh possibilities for understanding not only the text but themselves, the world, and God. The congregation is also a complex other manifesting its own culture (and multiple subcultures), which is made up of a collection of others who choose to be in relationship with one another and who—because of their otherness—perceive aspects of God and the Bible that the minister may miss. Toward this end, McClure proposes that the preacher bring members of the congregation actively into sermon preparation by participating in a "feed-forward" group (and also to attend to the congregation in feedback).[22] People, groups, and ideas beyond the congregation and beyond the church are others who often confront preacher and congregation with possibilities for understanding and life that have been altogether outside the ecclesial purview.

How Other Theologies Might Interpret Luke 7:11-17

The *confessional* preacher wants to know the distinct confession of faith in the biblical text.[23] Confession involves (1) essential elements of Christian tradition and (2) critical appropriation of those elements in view of the local context. The confessional perspective would likely (1) regard the essential elements of the text as the identity of Jesus Christ (portrayed by Luke) as a prophet in the tradition of Elijah and Elisha who brings (and is) God's transforming Word into the situation of death at Nain. But this preacher (2) recognizes that such events may not occur today in pragmatic experience exactly as reported by Luke. Nevertheless, the preacher recognizes that though cast in the language of an ancient worldview, the text asks us to believe and do and say that transforming Word is still present in situations of death. In the sermon the preacher might give a personal testimony of the Word transforming a situation like that at Nain.

When preaching on Luke 7:11-17, the *radically orthodox* would ponder how an encounter with the text would invite the congregation into participation in the divine life. The preacher could regard the text as an apple to offer to the hunger of the congregation. The incident in the text is a picture of the transformation that is at the heart of radical orthodoxy. When Jesus arrives at Nain, the brokenness in the community as a result of the death denies God's purpose for the elements of the community to live together in sacramental harmony. The preacher might help the congregation identify points at which secularism has left today's world as fractured as that of the widow, indeed, as effectively dead as her child. This preacher might regard the figure of Jesus as the incarnate One whose presence actualizes divine purposes. Indeed, Jesus is already present in the congregation with the transformational power depicted in the biblical passage. The preacher could hold up the occurrence at Nain as a paradigm of what happens when the congregation partakes of the Eucharist: the incarnate One present through the bread and the cup makes us alive and restores us to full participation in community. The sermon would invite the congregation to participate in similar life transformations taking place beyond the table and, indeed, beyond the boundaries of the congregation.

Preachers from the house of *otherness* likely would approach this text by giving attention to the motif of otherness but, befitting the emphasis on distinctiveness in this movement, preachers would do so with their own perspectives.[24] I offer only one way of calling attention to how dimensions of otherness confront the congregation through this passage. The young person is dead. Death is the ultimate expression of sameness, the final end of the particular, and appears to be the final (even universal) certainty. While the text focuses overtly on physical death, the multilayered literary style of Luke prompts the listener to consider other modes of death. Yet the otherness of Jesus introduces another possibility: the possibility of life. The world of the widow, and hence that of the listener, is not circumscribed by death. The encounter with Jesus as life-giving other implicitly urges the congregation to consider how encounters with others may have death-denying, life-affirming potential.

The text may arouse questions in listeners. If the sameness of death is not a certainty, then what other saming certainties are uncertain? On the one hand, this is a life-enlarging possibility for those whose lives are shaped by the powers of sameness that lead to death. On the other hand, the uncertainty of death may be a threat to those who seek to use it to enforce self-serving policies of sameness on others.

Questions for Other Theologies

The pragmatic approach of *confessional* preaching may sustain the community with respect to matters such as forgiveness, reconciliation, or being motivated to engage in mission. The congregation, after all, believes the confessions because the congregation's own faith is kindled or rekindled. But what happens when the tradition may lead the community to expect something (such as a divine intervention in history) that does not occur? What kind of theological foundation is necessary and sufficient? Furthermore, while this movement holds that the revelation of God in Christ is clearer than (but not superior to) that of the First Testament, the theological window is still left ajar for "clearer" to be taken, however unintentionally, for "a little better than."

From the preacher's point of view, a major question for preachers of *radical orthodoxy* is what their pervasive christological and trinitarian foci lead them to make of the First Testament. Indeed, the Bible has a low profile in radical orthodoxy. When the preacher of radical orthodoxy does turn to the Bible, the danger of eisegesis is lying at the door as the preacher is tempted to read later Christian formulations into the biblical text. Some Christians will be troubled by the claim of radical orthodoxy that their interpretation of creedalism is the *exclusive* antidote to secularism. From the point of view of accessibility, the literature of this first wave of radical orthodoxy is sufficiently dense that some readers will find it difficult to follow. Furthermore, at this point radical orthodoxy is available largely at the level of discourse among academics, and it is not entirely clear how radical orthodoxy would shape a living congregation.

A question for preachers whose formative category is *otherness* is how the preacher and congregation can relate to differing theological claims or ethical possibilities that arise from different biblical texts, different theological families, different communities, and different particular locations. To be sure, the preacher should respect the otherness of each, but when push comes to shove, how do a preacher and congregation identify those that are more and less trustworthy? Nor is it always clear when preacher or congregation should resist aspects of the otherness of others. What, if any, are the limits to expressions of diversity? Preachers and congregations of otherness thus are called to continual critical reevaluation, in dialogue with multiple others, regarding their perceptions of others.

Representative Readings

Allen, Charles W. "Radical Orthodoxy in the Parish, or Postmodern Critical Augustinianism for Dummies." *Encounter* 64 (2003): 219–29. Implications of radical orthodoxy for congregational life.

Allen, Ronald J. "Preaching and the Other." *Worship* 76 (2002): 211–24. Basic categories of otherness: text, congregation, God.

Florence, Anna Carter. *Preaching as Testimony.* Louisville: Westminster John Knox, 2007. Exquisite statement of otherness: preaching as giving testimony from one's particular theological and social location. Testimonial practices of women as paradigm.

Hogan, Lucy Lind. "Alpha, Omega, and Everything in Between: Toward a Postsecular Homiletics." In *Purposes of Preaching*, ed. Jana Childers, 67–82. St. Louis: Chalice , 2004. Though not endorsing radical orthodoxy, Lind Hogan gives sympathetic summary and identifies implications for preaching.

Lose, David. *Confessing Jesus Christ: Preaching in a Postmodern World.* Grand Rapids: Eerdmans, 2003. Preaching as confession.

McClure, John S. *Other-Wise Preaching: A Postmodern Ethic for Homiletics.* St. Louis: Chalice, 2001. The single most important work on otherness and preaching.

———. *The Roundtable Pulpit: Where Preaching and Leadership Meet.* Nashville: Abingdon, 1995. When the preacher brings laity into sermon preparation.

Rose, Lucy Atkinson. *Sharing the Word: Preaching in the Roundtable Church.* Louisville: Westminster John Knox, 1997. Preaching as conversation among different sources (others).

Smith, James K. A. *Introducing Radical Orthodoxy: Mapping a Post-Secular Theology.* Grand Rapids: Baker Academic, 2004. Basic orientation to radical orthodoxy.

Williams, Rowan. "The Sermon." In *Living the Eucharist: Affirming Catholicism Conference Papers.* Ed. Steven Conway and David Stancliffe, 44–55. London: Dartman, Longman, and Todd, 2001. Nascent radical orthodox perspective.

PART FOUR

Theological Movements Arising from Contextual Concerns

Thus far we have we have looked at theological movements that originated in large part to continue or adapt Enlightenment perspectives to theology (part 2) or began as reaction against aspects of the Enlightenment (part 3). However, many theologies originate without reference to the Enlightenment. Indeed, questions and issues raised by modernity are largely irrelevant to many preachers.

Issues emerging in particular cultural contexts are the points of origin of theologies considered in part 4. Liberation theologies (chap. 11) arise from matters of justice, dignity, equality, freedom, and access to material resources. The burning question for such theologies is more "How does God empower us in the face of massive threats to our quality of life and even survival?" and less "How can we have adequate grounds to believe that God exists?" Ethnic theologies (chap. 12) arise from the desire to understand God and the faithful life in terms drawn from particular ethnic cultures. Ethnic preachers resist the tendency arbitrarily to impose European categories and values on non-Western communities and interpretations of Christian faith.

These theological families are quite diverse, and many of them share concerns with theological houses already discussed. Preachers of liberation and mutual critical correlation, for instance, often come to similar conclusions regarding God's desire for people to live together in mutually supportive community. Indeed, liberation and ethnic themes sometimes interweave in ways that make these two categories artificial. Nevertheless, such categories have a heuristic value.

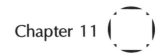

Chapter 11

Liberation Theologies and Preaching

Many preachers and congregations from all of the previously mentioned theological families seek liberation, for some preachers of every theological house want all individuals and communities to be free—liberated from the multiple forces that distort personal and communal existence, such as racism, gender discrimination, economic deprivation, ageism, absence of health care, exploitation, religious discrimination, and violence. However, about forty years ago a distinct theological movement burst into the ecclesial community called theology of liberation for whom the foregoing themes are the driving force. While liberation theologians share some foundational perspectives with other theological movements, liberation theology also has a distinct set of theological perspectives and a distinct theological method that this chapter will unfold.

As noted frequently in this book, preachers often cross the lines by which I have divided the main theological families. However, the crossover between liberation themes and the other families of theology is frequent. For instance, liberation theology found a sympathetic audience in those quarters of North America where themes from the social gospel (whose heyday was roughly 1900 to 1940) have lingered among preachers, with its emphasis on applying Christian principles to social issues, especially poverty, lack of education, poor health care, and labor reform.[1] Beyond the social gospel, as a process preacher for instance, I often speak of God's purposes as liberating, and I hear preachers from evangelical and postliberal circles speak similarly. I know many postliberal preachers who advocate the liberation of women just as I know evangelical preachers for whom racial justice is an urgent imperative. Nevertheless, liberation theology as such has distinct starting points, methods, and goals.

Liberation Theologies in Broad Outline

Liberation theology originated in Latin America among impoverished communities whose lives were restricted by economic and political oppression.[2] In liberation theology the notion of liberation refers in the immediate instance to individuals and communities becoming free of all arbitrary restrictions on human life. Liberation means release from all forms of oppression such as (but not limited to) racism, ethnic oppression, sexism, poverty, economic injustice, classism, heterosexism, ageism, colonialism, ecological destruction, political manipulation, nationalism, religious intolerance and persecution, and the unwarranted use of violence. Many liberationists see capitalism as especially heinous. Liberation theology seeks a material world in which all people live together in love, peace, respect, egalitarianism, and justice. In the liberated world all people have access to the material resources necessary for abundant living, and all individuals and communities have full and free opportunities to choose their own life-paths and to live in communities of mutual support. The concern of liberation theology is not limited to the material world, of course, but liberation preachers insist that salvation is incomplete without a change in material circumstances.

Liberation theologians typically interpret the Bible as the paradigmatic story of liberation with the exodus and the crucifixion and resurrection as key events. Leading to the exodus, the people of Israel were enslaved by Pharaoh, but God delivered them from bondage and established them as a community that was self-determining and that had abundant material resources (the land flowing with milk and honey). In the context of the oppressive Roman Empire, Jesus preached the realm of God, that is, a world of peace, justice, dignity, access to means of a secure livelihood, and free of the violence of Rome. The prospect of this new world so threatened the Jewish and Roman authorities that they put Jesus to death. However, God raised Jesus from the dead to reveal that the impulse toward liberation cannot be stopped.

While the exodus and the resurrection are the fundamental paradigms for understanding God's liberating purposes, preachers in the liberation family read much of the Bible as witnessing to God's aim to create just, fair, loving communities by dethroning oppressive powers (such as unjust and idolatrous rulers, exploitative members of the upper class, manipulative priests, and patriarchy). Indeed, liberation theologians tend to read the Bible as manifesting divine bias toward the poor, the outcast, and the marginalized. Some liberationists see God correspondingly rejecting the wealthy. The biblical text is often a model of how God is at work to liberate.

Liberation preachers recognize that oppression occurs because some groups in society have more power than others. Hence, for liberation to occur communities must respond with power. Consequently, preachers of liberation often turn to politics, economics, and other domains of power as means to liberation. Some liberation theologians regard violent social revolution as the only means to freedom, but others (such as liberation theologians inspired by Martin Luther King Jr.) insist that liberation must employ nonviolent (though unrelenting) strategies. Preachers in this movement often seek to help congregations recognize that God accomplishes many of God's purposes through social movements. The preacher then wants the congregation to become involved in social forces for liberation and thereby to join God at work.

Liberation theologians typically stress that the many forces of oppression are systemic in nature. Systemic oppression is not simply the behavior of individuals who choose to be oppressive but results from life-systems of values, expectations, and behaviors creating powerful force fields that shape individuals and groups and that control large segments of life. Systems of oppression are often linked so that they support one another. Individuals and groups often unconsciously serve systems. Individuals and groups can choose to resist systems but even as resistors they are still implicated in systemic oppression.

There are as many different kinds of liberation theology as there are forms of oppression. Advocates within particular strands of liberation theology typically concentrate on a particular oppression while recognizing the systemic interrelatedness of all forms of oppression.

African American Liberation Theologies

African American liberation theology focuses particularly on systemic racism and on the systemic connection of racism with other modes of oppression. These theologians point out that racism is more than a matter of prejudice by individuals of European origin against African Americans. Racism results from prejudice combined with the power to oppress and exploit African Americans. Racism is so deeply woven into life in the United States that it functions as a system that is beyond the control of any one individual but shapes attitudes and behaviors. Few Eurocentric people are conscious of its extent. African American preachers often call attention to "European privilege"—that is, the ways that life-systems in the United States favor people of European origin and disadvantage African Americans, for example in school curricula, hiring and employment practices, the legal system, health-care delivery, segregation in housing patterns, even the programs that appear in electronic media.

Theologians of African American liberation name forms and manifestations of racism and affirm that just as God liberated the slaves from Egypt, so God continues to work in liberating ways on behalf of African Americans (and other oppressed peoples today). They point out specific actions through which God is dismantling racism and working to create an antiracist/reconciling community. This theology seeks a fundamental redistribution of power and resources so that African Americans have a sense of personal and communal agency as well as access to resources to choose the kinds of lives that they want. African American liberation theology calls for the creation of systems that assert the dignity and worth of all and that guarantee opportunities for education, employment possibilities, the legal system, health-care delivery, and housing patterns.

Racism has so penetrated the United States that a Eurocentric person can never completely shed its privileges and can never be free of complicity with racist systems. Residents of the United States whose ancestors came from Europe are inherently and unavoidably racist. With respect to racism, the highest hope for a person of European origin is to be an antiracist racist, that is, to be a person who recognizes and resists racism.

If I may be permitted a personal comment, I am amazed that African American liberation theology, while bitterly lamenting the evil effects of racism, seldom calls for recrimination against people of European origin. Indeed, I am utterly astonished by the persistent call of much of this literature for a genuine national community in which people of European origin can live in solidarity with African Americans and other people of color. I assume this community spirit results from the depth of commitment among African American liberationists to God's ultimate hope to bless all peoples through life in covenantal community.

Feminist Liberation Theologies

A starting point for feminist liberation theology is male oppression (often as a part of other interlocking systems of oppression). Feminist liberation theologians expose manifestations of patriarchy and its destructive effects not only on women but on the whole human family. They name such things as uses of language that imply male superiority, practices in the church that relegate women to secondary status or that deny them opportunities for leadership, as well as gender discrimination in the workplace. Second, they identify how God's liberating purposes should be actively reshaping current social worlds in the direction of egalitarianism and mutuality.

Feminist liberation theologians advocate such things as the use of language that supports relationships of mutual solidarity, equal opportunities for women and men in serving congregations and in other aspects of leadership in the church, equal opportunities in all other spheres, and legal protections.

However, many feminists see liberation going far beyond equal access to spheres of power that have traditionally been dominated by males. They seek to reconstruct values, assumptions, norms, and patterns of relationship in the home, in churches, in the workplace, in schools, and in recreation. In particular, they urge the dismantling of hierarchical, linear, authoritarian patterns of male organizational behavior, as well as disfranchising good-ol'-boy networks that often exert informal but incredible shaping power in communities. Feminists further urge reshaping patterns of group life in all settings according to feminist values such as equality, fairness, collegiality, and respect for particularity.

Other Liberation Theologies
The following is a partial list of some of the other well-known liberation theologies in alphabetical order:[3]

- *Age*: typically focuses on discrimination against older people but sometimes focuses on discrimination against children and young people.

- *Asian*: focuses on discrimination against people of Asian origin; there are many different Asian ethnic and national liberation theologies.

- *Caribbean*: focuses on exploitation of people in the Caribbean, particularly by the United States but also by other developed nations.

- *Disability*: focuses on bias against people who are differently abled.

- *Gay and lesbian*: focuses on injustices against gay and lesbian persons.

- *U.S. Hispanic*: focuses on prejudice against Hispanic people in the United States.

- *Latin American*: focuses on economic, political, and other forms of injustice perpetrated against Latin Americans by the United States and other developed nations.

- *Mujerista*: focuses on multiple forms of oppression of women among U.S. Hispanic people and Latin Americans.

- *Womanist*: focuses on multiple forms of oppression of women in African American communities.

As noted at the outset of this chapter, many preachers combine liberation emphases with the themes of other theological houses.

Postcolonial Theology

Postcolonial theology shares many basic concerns of liberation theology, though its focus is particularly on peoples who have been subjected to colonial rule by Anglo-Europeans. Postcolonial theology seeks the liberation of formerly colonized continents, subcontinents, and nations from past and continuing political, economic, and social domination by people of European origin. Recognizing that social identity is constructed, postcolonial theology unmasks the fact that Europeans ascribe inferior status to inhabitants of colonized and formerly colonized lands. Many people in those areas continue to believe that European dominance is unavoidable, and some even internalize the ideas that Eurocentric culture is normative and that their own cultures are inferior. Postcolonial theory often uses the language of "subaltern" to describe the relationship of colonized peoples to their masters.[4] As a part of its liberating emphasis, postcolonial theology encourages formerly colonized peoples to reject European hegemony and to see themselves as human beings of full and complete stature from the perspective of their own distinctive cultural identities.

Purposes of Liberation Theology Sermons

The sermon from the perspective of this theological family has three basic tasks. The first task of the liberation sermon is to help the congregation name and understand the forces of oppression that are at work in the world of the congregation as well as in the interpretation of the Bible and in the Bible itself. Indeed, liberation preachers often approach situations and texts with a hermeneutic of suspicion. That is, liberation preachers seek to identify how particular interpretations of the Bible (and particular theological ideas) benefit some people to the detriment of others. An African American liberation preacher, for instance, might explore how preachers of European origin have misinterpreted a text in support of white privilege but how a different interpretation of the text points toward liberation.

The second function of the sermon is to help the congregation recognize where God is at work for liberation in today's world. Where does the preacher see a perspective, a social movement, or an individual initiative that has a liberating quality? What can the congregation anticipate in the way of positive change that will result from liberation? A feminist liberation preacher might expose how males have interpreted a text to reinforce male superiority, and also how a feminist can reinterpret the text as a charter for the liberation of women.

The third basic task of the message of liberation is to help the congregation identify how to respond appropriately to the liberating force field. For some congregations (or for some in the congregation), the news of liberation will point to welcome changes of circumstances. At one level, liberation means release from arbitrary restriction. On another level, liberation means empowerment and a sense of having agency. The sermon can help such folk identify ways that they can actively participate in the movement toward liberation. An African American or feminist preacher of liberation might help the congregation identify practical steps they can take to join in the movement toward emancipation.

However, some other congregations (or some in the congregation) benefit from the oppression of others and may actively or passively participate in maintaining systems of oppression. This is especially (though not exclusively) true of males of European origin. The sermon needs to help these people recognize their complicity in oppression, to repent, and to join in solidarity with those struggling toward a liberated world.

With respect to postcolonial preaching, the leading scholar of such preaching, Pablo Jiménez, asks, "Can the subaltern *preach?*" His answer is that such preaching is imperative. Its agenda is to "affirm that subaltern groups maintain cultural practices and 'texts' that empower them to deconstruct the false identity imposed by colonial rule." Indeed, Jiménez declares that the subaltern "has always been able to speak and that she or he has been constantly speaking (even though the colonial rulers disregarded or actively suppressed his or her voice)." Although postcolonial preaching theory is nascent, Jiménez sees it birthing a generation of preachers who are "poets, prophets, and pastors" in a liberating postcolonial mode.[5]

How Liberation Preachers Might Interpret Luke 7:11-17

The situation of the woman and the deceased young person is one of multiple forms of oppression. With the death of the young person, the widow is left alone. Given the patriarchal character of ancient society, the woman was in a marginalized state. With the death of her only child, she likely would receive no inheritance but would depend upon the community to provide for her. The death has diminished her material world. The liberation preacher would want to know particularly how women in the world of the congregation are in positions similar to the widow at Nain and in the systemic forces that force women into such circumstances.

The text does not say why the young person died, but death is here as the archetypal act of oppression. While the liberation preacher is certainly interested in the figurative dimensions of death in this text, this preacher may also be very interested in circumstances that result in physical death today, for instance, genocide, war, torture, unsafe and exploitative labor practices, poverty, abuse, and lack of health care.

For Luke, Jesus is the agent of the realm of God. This text illustrates Jesus' mission for the realm voiced in Luke 4:18-19 (an important text to many liberation theologians). By raising the decedent, Jesus demonstrates that the realm is more powerful than the forces that put the young person to death. Furthermore, the raising regenerates a measure of the social power of the woman, and also restores her place in community. However, the liberation preacher may decry the fact that Jesus does not here challenge the basic structures of patriarchy but only returns the woman to them. Nevertheless, there are impulses in the text toward something more. Jesus has compassion for the woman in the same way that Luke records compassion for males (Luke 10:33; 15:20). While the miracle at Nain did not completely restore the life of the woman to Edenic egalitarianism, Jesus' actions anticipate a time (the social world of the realm) when women will, as in Eden, again be full and equal partners in community.

Questions for Liberation Preaching

Occasional liberation preachers reduce God's concerns to social and political emancipation, overlooking God's concern for all other aspects of life. Moreover, preachers of liberation sometimes view God's purposes in bifurcated terms as entirely in favor of the oppressed and entirely against oppressors. Indeed, a subtle vengefulness sometimes creeps into liberation theology. However, increasing numbers of liberation theologians believe oppressors are themselves oppressed by their own oppression so that the liberation of the oppressed can also mean the liberation of repentant oppressors who join the movement toward liberation. Oppressive systems need to go, but people who have been co-opted by those systems can be redeemed at least to the extent that they repent and resist the oppressive system. When interpreting the Second Testament, liberation theologians often portray the Jewish people (and even the Torah) as rigid, legalistic, and manipulative. Jesus liberates people from oppressive Judaism (especially the Pharisees). This way of thinking reinforces anti-Judaism and even anti-Semitism.

Representative Readings

Black, Kathy. *A Healing Homiletic: Preaching and Disability.* Nashville: Abingdon, 1996. Preaching from disability perspective.

Bond, L. Susan. *Trouble with Jesus: Women, Christology, and Preaching.* St. Louis: Chalice, 1999. Feminist, womanist, and *mujerista* perspectives.

Burghardt, Walter J. *Preaching the Just Word.* New Haven: Yale University Press, 1997. Focuses on the poor, oppressed, and marginalized.

Childs, James M. Jr., *Preaching Justice: The Ethical Vocation of Word and Sacrament Ministry.* Valley Forge: Trinity International, 2000. Justice is at the core of God's concern, with particular attention to racism and greed.

González, Justo L., and Catherine G. González, *The Liberating Pulpit.* Nashville: Abingdon, 2003. Classic text for liberation perspective.

Harris, James Henry. *Preaching Liberation.* Fortress Resources for Preaching. Minneapolis: Fortress Press, 1995. Pays particular attention to African American experience.

———. *The Word Made Plain: The Power and Promise of Preaching.* Minneapolis: Fortress Press, 2004. Philosophical approach to liberation theology with African American lens.

Jiménez, Pablo. "Toward a Postcolonial Homiletic: Justo L. González's Contribution to Hispanic Preaching." In *Hispanic Christian Thought at the Dawn of the Twenty-First Century: Apuntes in Honor of Justo L. González.* Ed. Alvin Padilla, Robert Goizueta, Eldin Villafañe, 159–67. Nashville: Abingdon, 2005. Foundational essay on a postcolonial homiletic.

McGee, Lee. *Wrestling with the Patriarchs: Retrieving Women's Voices in Preaching.* Abingdon Preacher's Library. Nashville: Abingdon, 1996. Issues for women preachers regarding identity and voice.

Smith, Christine M. *Preaching as Weeping, Confession, and Resistance: Radical Response to Radical Evil.* Louisville: Westminster John Knox, 1991. Handicapism, ageism, sexism, heterosexism, racism, and classism.

———. *Weaving the Sermon: Preaching in a Feminist Perspective.* Louisville: Westminster John Knox , 1989. Pivotal feminist text.

Turner, Mary Donovan, and Mary Lin Hudson. *Saved from Silence: Finding Women's Voice in Preaching.* St. Louis: Chalice, 1999. Women on finding voice as liberating.

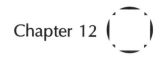

Chapter 12

Ethnic Theologies and Preaching

Changes in language preferences make it difficult to title this chapter. A few years ago, I probably would have called it "Racial and Ethnic Theologies", or "Minority Theologies." However, communities should decide the names by which they are known. My impression is that in recent years, the communities to which these designations refer have moved away from language of minority and race and have moved toward the language of ethnicity.

In any event, I use the term *ethnic* to refer to people from cultures of non-European origin, such as African, African American, Asian, Asian American, Hispanic American (in the United States and Canada), Latin American, and Native American. In today's pluralistic world, some people may identify with more than one such community. I use the double expressions—for instance, both African and African American—because ethnic communities located in North America often experience their culture of origin differently from those in the homeland. Indeed, such folk often feel exiled in North America and must negotiate two (or more) cultures.

Ethnic Theologies in Broad Outline

Attitudes of European Christians (and of Christians of European descent in North America) toward the relationship of Christian faith and culture are in the backdrop of the emergence of ethnic theologies. For a long time, many Europeans assumed that Christian faith and European culture went hand in hand, as evidenced in missionary movements conducted by these churches of European origin, especially in the nineteenth and early twentieth centuries.

79

In the last seventy-five years, this situation has changed. Most importantly, many non-Europeans have discovered that the languages, values, and practices of their own cultures provide categories that better help members of those cultures embrace a Christian vision other than those imported from Europe or North America. Moreover, increasing numbers of persons with Eurocentric viewpoints recognize that all understandings of Christian faith are expressed in the language of particular cultures. Some theologians and preachers of European origin once assumed, at least tacitly, that their understanding of Christian faith was relatively pure, relatively objective, and relatively free of cultural representation. However, increasing numbers of preachers of European origin recognize that all thought and communication partake of cultural presuppositions and expressions. All awareness is culturally conditioned and interpretive. As Korean theologian Andrew Sung Park notes, no culture is entirely Christian.[1]

Ethnic theologies are often correlational in that preachers correlate pivotal ideas and practices from the Bible and Christian tradition with ideas and practices in the culture. Such preachers translate basic Christian themes and practices into thought-forms and actions familiar to the culture. Beyond correlation, however, some ethnic theologies compare and contrast Christian ideas and practices with thoughts and customs in the culture. Indeed, some ethnic preachers use the perspective of the culture to adapt and even criticize motifs from the Bible and Christian tradition. Occasional ethnic preachers find assumptions and actions from the culture to be superior to traditional Christian perspectives.

One must consider each ethnic theology in its own right to ascertain the degree to which an approach is correlational or goes beyond correlation to reformulation. There can be as many ethnic theologies and approaches to preaching as there are ethnic communities. Indeed, we now see multicultural theologies.[2] A short chapter cannot deal with the specific content of so many different approaches. We can, however, illustrate how some ethnic preachers might interpret selected categories from the Bible (and Christian tradition) in the language, imagery, mores, and practices of the preacher's ethnic culture. To illustrate, I report how some Korean preachers in North America associate Korean cultural values and Christian notions.

- *Patterns of mental operation.* Eurocentric people often think in dualistic terms of either/or. Much of the Bible assumes such a perspective, for instance, wise or foolish, saved or condemned. The Korean mind, however, can hold multiple perspectives in creative relationship without resorting to mutual exclusion.

Indeed, Korean thinking is inclusive, accepting "the ambivalent reality of one-in-many and many-in-one," a "multiplex mode of thinking." A sermon, consequently, can be open ended.[3]

- *Key points of identification between biblical contexts and the ethnic culture.* Many Korean congregations in North America find themselves in a situation of exile or even persecution. Many Koreans experience discrimination and even rejection. In this respect, they experience *han,* the pervasive sense of suffering that has characterized Korean people for several centuries as they struggled in the homeland under occupation by the Chinese and Japanese and as immigrants continue to struggle in North America with discrimination, economic insecurity, social inequity, and other distortions.[4] Second-generation Koreans in North America sometimes feel as though they are in a no-man's-land as they feel neither fully Korean nor fully inculturated into North America. Many Korean Americans are uncertain how to maintain ethnic identity while dealing with the larger (and sometimes hostile) culture.

- *Key points of interaction between the ethnic culture and biblical language, imagery, and ideas.* Shamanism is part of the "internal character" of Korean culture. The shaman interprets messages from the gods that release people from suffering. Christian preaching resonates with this belief by promising relief to the *minjung* (suffering people). The preacher and worship leaders are often "shamanistic in belief and behavior."[5] Eunjoo Mary Kim finds that Jesus' death and resurrection and the promise of a final eschatological victory resonates with traditional Korean religion to provide an "eschatological spirituality" that empowers life in the present by providing hope for the future.[6]

The preceding categories are only examples of interactions between the Bible (and other Christian sources) and ethnic cultures. Other categories include how we know God, sources of authority (especially character and function of the Bible), the nature and mission of God, Christ, the Holy Spirit, purposes of human life, relationship of human life and the natural world, basic problems besetting humankind and nature, the purpose of the church, redemption, and the relationship of Christianity to other religions.

Some ethnic theologies contain themes that resonate with theological themes discussed in parts 2 and 3. Some ethnic theologians, for instance, assume some evangelical perspectives even while theologizing in patterns of thought that are characteristic of indigenous culture.

Moreover, some ethnic preachers do not share the inclination to interpret the Christian faith in categories of their cultures of origin. Indeed, occasional preachers in ethnic settings interpret Christian faith in European terms. To continue the Korean example, Kim notices that some Korean ministers in the United States drift away from the eschatological hope for a new world (free of discrimination, injustice, social inequity, and suffering) and instead preach a version of the American dream.[7]

Purposes of Sermons in Ethnic Communities

Ethnic preachers tend to state the purpose of the sermon in ways that are consistent with that culture's understanding of the purpose of the church in relationship to its social context. However, we may generally think of the purpose of a sermon in an ethnic community as helping the community come to an adequate understanding of the presence and purposes of God in language, imagery, and other forms of expression that are appropriate both to core Christian affirmations (and moral behaviors) and also to the culture of the community.

Depending upon the situation of the community and the perspective of the preacher, the purpose of the sermon may take one of the following aims: (1) to find a correlation between a biblical text or a Christian affirmation and the community, or a translation from the language and practices of the Bible and Christian tradition into the language and practices of the culture; (2) to correlate some aspects of a text or Christian idea or practice with the culture while criticizing other aspects; (3) to find in the culture an idea or practice that seems superior to a perspective in Christian tradition; or (4) to criticize an aspect of the culture that is not compatible with the Christian vision.

Ethnic preachers often develop and embody sermons in ways that are shaped by their cultural heritage. The preacher does not simply put on cultural forms in the same way that I put on a coat to go outside in winter. When I take off the coat, I am unchanged. Rather, where communication in cultural ideas and feelings occurs, form and meaning shape one another. When the preacher uses cultural forms, the deep resonance of the culture is invoked over the sermon while the sermon addresses the culture.

African American Preaching in Ethnic Perspective

Much African American preaching emphasizes themes that are found in liberation theology. However, as pointed out by Henry H. Mitchell, dean of African American scholars of preaching, not all African American preachers subscribe to the assumptions and methods of liberation theology in a formal way. Indeed, Mitchell finds that many African American ministers preach from a "soul theology," that is, an ethnic folk system of beliefs. The main themes of soul theology are

- the providence of God,

- the justice of God,

- the majesty, omnipotence, and omniscience of God,

- the goodness of God and creation,

- the grace of God,

- the equality and uniqueness of persons,

- the family of God as the whole of humankind,

- the importance of perseverance.[8]

Such themes are sympathetic to leading liberation concerns, but preachers often frame them without relying specifically on the perspectives or methods of liberation theology. Many African American preachers, of course, weave together liberation and soul themes.

Mitchell further identifies characteristics of much African American preaching that reverberate with the cultural life and traditional religion of West Africa. These associations include the tonal quality of patterns of speech (with soft, velvet qualities), call and response, the use of colorful language, embodiment (delivery) that is expressive, the use of stories that teach moral behavior and how to cope with life, preference for concrete speech over abstract thought and expression that uses the biblical traditions in an oral way, imaginative elaboration of a story from the Bible, ecstatic moments and a celebratory climax to the sermon (for instance, the preacher's joyous and sonorous expostulation sometimes called whooping) leading to contagion, and the preacher developing a personal flair.[9] These things are more than matters of style. When these things occur, the congregation intuitively participates not only in aspects of West African religion and culture but invokes key dimensions of the African American cultural experience.

How Ethnic Preachers Might Interpret Luke 7:11-17

As we said in connection with the purposes of preaching among ethnic congregations, different ethnic preachers will interpret the story of the widow at Nain according to the leading perspectives of the preacher's culture. If the preacher seeks to effect a correlation between the biblical story and the culture, the preacher would seek positive points of contact between the elements of the text and the culture.

In that spirit, many preachers would consider issues such as the ones below. A reader can add the phrase "if anything" to almost any questions in the following.

- What, if anything, is the significance of death in the culture?

- What does the disruption of relationship by death (such as that between the mother and the young person, and between the widow and the larger community) mean in the culture?

- Who or what in the culture functions as a healing presence in the way represented by the figure of Jesus in the text?

- What, if anything, is the significance of the raising of a dead person both as a physical action and as a figurative action?

- More generally, what do miracles indicate in the culture?

- How does the culture perceive widows? What is the social and economic impact of death?

- What is the responsibility of the community to continue to work miracles in the way portrayed in the text?

- Do values that are in the background of the story (such as shame and honor or clean and unclean) function in the culture?

- How does the designation *prophet* intersect with the culture?

- What would this story signal to the congregation regarding what they might expect from God in their immediate worlds and in the future?

Questions for Ethnic Theologies

The biggest question for ethnic theologies and preaching is the degree to which the interchange between biblical motifs and the culture of the community is faithful to both Christian theology and the cultural expression. Of course, a correlation is never a perfect fit, but a preacher can either lose touch with Christian orientation or can impose a Christian perspective onto a cultural embodiment in such a way as to violate the integrity of the cultural element. At the risk of cultural insensitivity, I would also raise the related question of the degree to which ethnic congregations function to preserve ethnic identity and to foster growth in Christian discipleship and witness.

This issue prompts an observation and a possibility. Many preachers in congregations of the long-established churches of European orgin in North American are so aware of the distance between Christian vision and prevailing cultural mores, and so fond of speaking of the church as a countercultural community, that we give very little attention to the possibility of finding some positive correlation between cultural and Christian values and practices. Is it possible that beneath the glitz, individualism, materialism, exploitation, and violence of conventional middle-class culture among people of European origin, a preacher might identify some points of positive correlation with the gospel?

Representative Readings

Note: Liberation themes resonate in many of these resources.

Bond, L. Susan. *Contemporary African American Preaching: Diversity in Theory and Style.* St. Louis: Chalice, 2003. Nine leading African American preachers.

Cannon, Katie Geneva. *Teaching Preaching: Isaac Rufus Clark and Black Sacred Rhetoric.* New York: Continuum, 1995. Lifts up the approach of I. R. Clark.

Crawford, Evans. *The Hum: Call and Response in African American Preaching.* Abingdon Preacher's Library. Nashville: Abingdon, 1995. Participatory style in preaching.

Fry Brown, Teresa. *Weary Throats and New Songs: Black Women Proclaiming God's Word.* Nashville: Abingdon, 2003. African American women's experience.

González, Justo, and Pablo Jiménez, *Púlpito: An Introduction to Hispanic Preaching.* Nashville: Abingdon, 2005. Foundational orientation to Hispanic preaching in English.

Kim, Eunjoo Mary. *Preaching the Presence of God: A Homiletic from an Asian American Perspective.* Valley Forge: Judson, 1999. The presence of God as a leading motif in Asian American preaching.

Larue, Cleophus J. *Power in the Pulpit: How America's Most Effective Black Preachers Prepare Their Sermons.* Louisville: Westminster John Knox, 2002. Title is self-explanatory.

———. *The Heart of Black Preaching.* Louisville: Westminster John Knox, 1999. Title is self-explanatory.

Lee, Jung Young. *Korean Preaching: An Interpretation.* Nashville: Abingdon, 1997. Main lines of Korean preaching.

Mitchell, Ella P., ed. *Those Preachin' Women: Sermons by Black Women Preachers.* Valley Forge: Judson, 1985, 1988, 1996, 2004. 4 vols. Anthologies of sermons by dynamic African American women.

——. *Women: To Preach or Not to Preach. Twenty-One Outstanding Black Preachers Say Yes.* Valley Forge: Judson, 1991. Includes sermons from Vashti McKenzie, Cynthia L. Hale, and Bishop Barbara Harris.

Mitchell, Henry H. *Black Folk Belief: Folk Beliefs of Blacks in America and West Africa.* New York: Harper & Row, 1975. Summary of main lines of beliefs of many people in the pews.

——. *Black Preaching: Introduction to a Powerful Art.* Nashville: Abingdon, 1999. Pivotal work on the history of African American preaching, preparation of African American preachers, and characteristics of African American preaching.

——, and Nicholas Cooper-Lewter. *South Theology: The Heart of American Black Culture.* Nashville: Abingdon, 1992 (o.p. 1986). Presentation of local theology typical of many African American communities.

Na, Koo Yong. "Preaching and Cultural Context: A Case Study in Preaching in a Korean Context." In *Preaching in the Context of Worship.* Ed. David M. Greenhaw and Ronald J. Allen, 129–45. St. Louis: Chalice, 2000.

Smith, Christine Marie. *Preaching Justice: Ethnic and Cultural Perspectives.* Cleveland: United Church Press, 1998. Eight perspectives: disability, Native American, Womanist, Filipino, Hispanic, Korean, Jewish, and lesbian.

Thomas, Frank. *They Like to Never Quit Praisin' God: The Role of Celebration in Preaching.* Cleveland: Pilgrim, 1997. Designing the sermon to reach climactic theological celebration of God's presence and power.

Reprise

This book describes the broad lines of eleven theological families and the preaching that follows from them. These families and their characteristics appear on table 1, which summarizes each family's basic theological concern, attitude toward the Bible, basic theological method, and understanding of the purposes of preaching.

Table 2 correlates historical and contemporary theological families. As that page and chapter 2 remind readers, a preacher often intermingles themes from historical theological perspectives with those of contemporary theological families. For instance, as indicated on table 2, my approach to preaching combines elements of the Reformed family with process theology. I follow the Reformed tradition in thinking that a basic function of the sermon is to teach, while actually interpreting the Bible and teaching from the perspective of process theology.

In the introduction, I hypothesized that many preachers would read the descriptions of the theological families in this book and think, "I do not fit neatly into just one of these theological families. My theology and my preaching contain qualities from different theological families." As this volume closes, let me reemphasize that my interest is not in imposing artificial labels but in helping preachers recognize the similarities between their own approaches to preaching and these families.

I hope that coming face to face with clear descriptions of different theological families will help a preacher identify the ones that the preacher finds more and less credible and attractive, and why the preacher finds them so. In this respect the book serves as an aid to learning.

Such critical self-consciousness can help preachers optimize the strengths of their particular approaches to theology and preaching as well as reflect on questions and weak points. When a preacher fits in more than one box on tables 1 or 2, a preacher can name the families to which the preacher belongs, locate the preacher's center of gravity, and reflect on how the preacher can relate to the various families so as to avoid contradiction that may occur as the preacher brings together different families.

This book may also help ministers recognize why other preachers develop sermons the way they do. In my classes in preaching, we read (or listen to on recording or watch on video) sermons by other preachers. Nearly always a student will burst out, "Now I know why that preacher makes the moves that she makes." Such awareness can help a preacher think clearly about what seems appealing and not appealing about other ministers' sermons. It can also help ministers think about the degree to which they might like to adapt something of the approach of another preacher in the course of developing their own voices.

	Basic concern of this theological family	Attitude toward the Bible	Basic theological method	Purposes of preaching
Liberal	Find a faith compatible in modern worldview	Bible human interpretation of divine activity	Correlation of biblical text or doctrine with today	To translate biblical text into worldview of today
Mutual Critical Correlation	Seek a faith honoring core of tradition while critical of implausible elements	Bible a library of views, some trustworthy but others less so	Mutual critical correlation between text and today	Explore mutual critical correlation to clarify what they can believe and do
Process	Articulate continuing Christian core in process perception of world	Perspectives from ancient worldviews on God's power and purposes	Bring propositions from Bible into dialogue with process philosophy	Conversation among proposals; congregation chooses one that makes sense
Evangelical	Bring people into church as ark of salvation	Bible is factual record of God's activity	Clarify what Bible says	Discover meaning of Bible and apply to today
Neoorthodox	Encounter and respond to Word of God	Encounter with Bible releases God's Word	Interpret Bible as God's Word	Confront congregation with God's Word
Postliberal	Develop Christian identity, practice, and witness	Bible is source of Christian identity and practice	Redescribe world from perspective of Bible	Help congregation develop Christian identity
Confessional	Understand confessions as believable for congregation	Bible is series of confessions	Identify what text confesses	Help folk believe and act on confession in text
Radical Orthodoxy	Reject secularism and return to orthodoxy via postmodern philosophy	Bible contains assertions of orthodox Christian theology	Recover orthodox affirmations to overcome emptiness of secularism	Help congregation participate in divine life toward transformation
Otherness	Encourage congregation to respect others	Bible is library of others	Attend to possibilities raised by others	Consider how text leads to respect others
Liberation	Call for world of love, peace, justice, abundance	Bible is record of God's liberating work	Identify oppression and liberation in world today	Help congregation join movement to liberation
Ethnic	Discover how Christian faith relates to ethnic culture	Bible is key to Christian understanding but is itself a cultural expression	Often seeks to correlate text with culture, but can criticize text or culture	Help congregation discover how Bible and culture interpret each other

TABLE ONE — Comparing Key Motifs in Different Theological Families

TABLE TWO — Correlating Historical and Contemporary Theological Families

This table indicates possible intersections between historic and contemporary theological families. Historic families are listed across the top and contemporary families down the side. I have entered my own name as an example.

	Orthodox	Roman Catholic	Lutheran	Anglican/ Episcopalian	Reformed	Wesleyan	Anabaptist/ Baptist	Friends	Pentecostal
Liberal									
Mutual Critical Correlation									
Process					Ron Allen				
Evangelical									
Neoorthodox									
Postliberal									
Confessional									
Radical Orthodoxy									
Otherness									
Liberation									
Ethnic									

Notes

Introduction

1. For preaching on biblical themes, see Ronald J. Allen, *Wholly Scripture: Preaching Biblical Themes* (St. Louis: Chalice, 2004). For preaching on topics (doctrines, practices, personal and social issues) see Ronald J. Allen, *Preaching the Topical Sermon* (Louisville: Westminster John Knox, 1992), and Jane Rzepka and Ken Sawyer, *Thematic Preaching: An Introduction* (St. Louis: Chalice, 2001).

Chapter 1 • Theology Shapes Preaching

1. An excellent guide for sorting out such things is Burton Z. Cooper and John S. McClure, *Claiming Theology in the Pulpit* (Louisville: Westminster John Knox, 2003).

2. This observation is truer of preachers in Protestant and Roman Catholic communities than of the various Orthodox churches. While preachers from all three movements regard themselves as representatives of particular traditions, the Orthodox churches tend to place more emphasis on the preacher as a voice of tradition and less emphasis on the preacher's own creativity. See the discussion of Orthodox preaching in chap. 2, 9–10.

Chapter 2 • Historic Theologies Still Shape Preaching

1. "Constitution of the Sacred Liturgy: Article 7" in *The Documents of Vatican II*, ed. Walter M. Abbott (New York: Association, 1966), 40–41; for other references to preaching in the documents of Vatican II, see 47, 116, 125, 127, 149, 269, 405, 418, 440, 454, 472, 535, 539–40, 591, 694.

2. Mary Catherine Hilkert, *Naming Grace: Preaching and the Sacramental Imagination* (New York: Continuum, 1997), 16, 72, 88.

3. Robert P. Waznack, "Homily," in *The New Dictionary of Sacramental Worship*, ed. Peter E. Fink (Collegeville: Liturgical, 1990), 552–58. These ideas are developed fully in: Bishops' Committee on Priestly Life and Ministry, National Conference of Catholic Bishops, *Fulfilled In Your Hearing: The Homily in the Sunday Assembly* (Washington, D.C.: Office of Publishing Services, United States Catholic Conference, 1982).

4. Consultation on Common Texts, *The Revised Common Lectionary* (Nashville: Abingdon, 1992).

5. John Wesley, *John Wesley's Works*, ed. Albert C. Outler (Nashville: Abingdon, 1984), 1:104.

6. Charles Wesley, "Love Divine, All Loves Excelling," in *The Chalice Hymnal*. (St. Louis: Chalice, 1995), 517.

7. Walter B. Shurden, *The Baptist Identity: Four Fragile Freedoms* (Macon: Smith and Helwys, 1997), 4. I am grateful to Robert Stephen Reid for this reference.

Chapter 3 • The Enlightenment

1. On premodern, modern, and postmodern worldviews, see Ronald J. Allen, Scott Black Johnston, and Barbara Shires Blaisdell, *Theology for Preaching: Authority, Truth and Knowledge of God in a Postmodern Ethos* (Nashville: Abingdon, 1997).

2. William C. Placher, *Unapologetic Theology* (Louisville: Westminster John Knox, 1989), 26.

3. Friedrich Schleiermacher, *On Religion: Speeches to Its Cultured Despisers*, ed. Richard Crofter, Cambridge Texts in Religion and Philosophy (Cambridge: Cambridge University Press, 1996).

4. Schleiermacher's critics today often miss the fact that his underlying purpose was apologetic and even evangelistic. He wanted to show that a credible and lively religious faith was possible and, in fact, was important for the human being to develop fully. Indeed, human beings are impoverished when they are not religious.

5. Schleiermacher, *On Religion*, 36.

6. Ibid.

Chapter 4 • Liberal Theology and Preaching

1. Rudolf Bultmann, "New Testament and Mythology," in *Kerygma and Myth*, ed. Hans Werner Bartsch, trans. Reginald H. Fuller (New York: Harper & Row, 1961), 1–44.

2. Personal correspondence, 2006. Cf. Nancy Lammers Gross, *If You Cannot Preach Like Paul . . . .* (Grand Rapids: Eerdmans, 2002), 75–87.

Chapter 5 • Theology of Mutual Critical Correlation and Preaching

1. Paul Tillich, *Systematic Theology*, 3 vols. in 1 (Chicago: University of Chicago Press, 1967), 1:60–64. Tillich could be discussed as a liberal, but I place him at the outset of the discussion of mutual critical correlation because many of the early theologians of mutual critical correlation began as Tillichians or drew from Tillich.

2. David Tracy, *The Analogical Imagination: Christian Theology and the Culture of Pluralism* (New York: Crossroad, 1981), 24–27, 60–61, 64, 80, 374–76, 405–8, 419, 447.

Chapter 6 • Process Theology and Preaching

1. Clark M. Williamson and Ronald J. Allen, *Adventures of the Spirit: A Guide to Worship from the Perspective of Process Theology* (Lanham: University Press of America, 1997), 48–49.

2. Paul Tillich is a theologian who built a theology around the category of being. See his *Systematic Theology*, 3 vols. in 1 (Chicago: University of Chicago Press, 1967), esp. 2:10–12.

3. Williamson and Allen, *Adventures of the Spirit*, 49.

4. Alfred North Whitehead, *Process and Reality*, corrected ed., ed. David Ray Griffin and Donald W. Sherburne (New York: Free, 1978), 42.

5. Marjorie Hewitt Suchocki, *The Fall to Violence: Original Sin in Relational Theology* (New York: Continuum, 1994), 66.

6. Ibid.

7. John B. Cobb Jr., "The Authority of the Bible," in *The Hermeneutics and Worldliness of Faith*, ed. Charles Courtney, Olin Ivey, and Gordon Michelson, *The Drew Gateway* 45 (1975): 200.

8. Whitehead, *Process and Reality*, 259.

9. Bruce G. Epperly, "Miracles without Supernaturalism," *Encounter* 67 (2006): 54–55.

Chapter 7 • Evangelical Theology and Preaching

1. On the complex of factors eventuating in fundamentalism, see George M. Marsden, *Fundamentalism and American Culture: The Shaping of American Evangelicalism 1870–1925* (New York: Oxford University Press, 1980). On fundamentalist movements more broadly, see *The Fundamentalism Project*, multiple volumes, ed. Martin E. Marty and R. Scott Appleby (Chicago: University of Chicago Press, 1994ff.).

2. J. I. Packer, "Introduction: Why Preach?" *The Preacher and Preaching*, ed. Samuel T. Logan Jr. (Phillipsburg: Presbyterian and Reformed, 1986), 8.

3. John R. W. Stott, *The Contemporary Christian Applying God's Word to Today's World* (Downers Grove: InterVarsity, 1995), 208.

4. Haddon W. Robinson, *Biblical Preaching: The Development and Delivery of Expository Messages* (Grand Rapids: Baker, 1980), 18.

Chapter 8 • Neoorthodox Theology and Preaching

1. Barth cited in William H. Willimon, *Conversations with Barth on Preaching* (Nashville: Abingdon, 2006), 143.

2. Karl Barth, *The Humanity of God* (Philadelphia: Westminster, 1960).

3. Karl Barth, "*Nein*: Answer to Emil Brunner," in Barth, *Natural Theology* (London: Centenary, 1946), 65–128.

4. Karl Barth, *Church Dogmatics*, I/1: *Doctrine of the Word of God: Prolegomena to Church Dogmatics*, trans. G. T. Thompson (Edinburgh: T&T Clark, 1936), 61 (short references hereafter cited in this style: I/1, 61).

5. Ibid., I/1, 106.

6. Karl Barth, *The Preaching of the Gospel*, trans. B. E. Hooke (Philadelphia: Westminster, 1963), 64–65.

7. Karl Barth, *Church Dogmatics*, IV/2: *Doctrine of Reconciliation: Jesus Christ the Servant as Lord*, trans. G. W. Bromiley (Edinburgh: T&T Clark, 1958), 211.

8. Karl Barth, *Church Dogmatics*, III/2: *The Doctrine of Creation: The Creature*, trans. H. Knight, G. W. Bromiley, J. K. S. Reid, R. H. Fuller (Edinburgh: T&T Clark, 1960), 211.

9. Barth, *Church Dogmatics*, IV/2, 226–27.

10. Karl Barth, *Church Dogmatics*, IV/1: *The Doctrine of Reconciliation*, trans. G. W. Bromiley (Edinburgh: T&T Clark, 1956), 334.

11. Barth, *Church Dogmatics*, IV/2, 200; Barth, *Church Dogmatics*, IV/3: *Doctrine of Reconciliation: Jesus Christ the True Witness*, trans. G. W. Bromiley (Edinburgh: T&T Clark, 1961), 49.

12. Barth, *Church Dogmatics*, III/2, 62.

13. Ibid., III/2, 497; IV/2, 176.

Chapter 9 • Postliberal Theology and Preaching

1. Hans Frei, *The Eclipse of Biblical Narrative* (New Haven: Yale University Press, 1974); Frei, *The Identity of Jesus Christ: The Hermeneutical Bases of Dogmatic Theology* (Philadelphia: Fortress Press, 1975).

2. George A. Lindbeck, *The Nature of Doctrine Religion and Theology in a Postliberal Age* (Philadelphia: Westminster John Knox, 1984), 35.

3. Stanley Hauerwas and William Willimon, *Resident Aliens: Life in the Christian Colony* (Nashville: Abingdon, 1988).

4. Hauerwas and Willimon, *Resident Aliens*, 24; authors' emphasis.

5. Charles L. Campbell, *Preaching Jesus Christ: New Directions for Homiletics in Hans Frei's Postliberal Theology* (Grand Rapids: Eerdmans, 1997), 228; my italics. See further Frei, *Identity of Jesus Christ*, 155–57.

6. Campbell, *Preaching Jesus Christ*, 225.

7. Ibid., 224.

8. On the intertwining of Christian practices in different aspects of congregational identity, see Ronald J. Allen, *Preaching and Practical Ministry*, Preaching and Its Partners (St. Louis: Chalice, 2001).

9. Richard Lischer, "Preaching as the Church's Language," in *Listening to the Word: Studies in Honor of Fred B. Craddock*, ed. Gail R. O'Day and Thomas G. Long, (Nashville: Abingdon, 1993), 113–14.

10. For a postliberal consideration of how to preach exorcisms and miracle stories, with special reference to the debilitating circumstances in the miracle stories as principalities and powers in the Hellenistic age, see Charles L. Campbell, *The Word before the Powers: An Ethic of Preaching* (Louisville: Westminster John Knox, 2002), 54–58. "Jesus' ministry . . . involves a thoroughgoing challenge and alternative to the principalities and powers of the world. [Jesus] lives free of the powers' clutches and enacts a radical alternative to their ways of domination and death" (57).

11. I express thanks to Charles Campbell for this observation (personal correspondence).

Chapter 10 • Other Theologies and Preaching

1. David J. Lose, *Confessing Jesus Christ: Preaching in a Postmodern World* (Grand Rapids: Eerdmans, 2003), 40.

2. Ibid., 53, 43.

3. Ibid., 80.

4. Ibid., 91.

5. John Milbank, Graham Ward, and Catherine Pickstock, "Introduction," in *Radical Orthodoxy: A New Theology*, ed. Milbank, Ward, and Pickstock (London and New York: Routledge, 1999), 1.

6. Ibid.

7. Ibid., 2.

8. Ibid., 1, 2.

9. Ibid., 2.

10. Charles W. Allen, "Radical Orthodoxy in the Parish or Postmodern Critical Augustinianism for Dummies," *Encounter* 64 (2003): 14.

11. Emmanuel Lévinas, *Totality and Infinity*, trans. Alphonso Lingus (Pittsburgh: Duquesne University Press, 1969), 37.

12. Lose, *Confessing Jesus Christ*. 111.

13. Ibid., 107.

14. Lose, personal correspondence, 2007.

15. Lose, *Confessing Jesus Christ*. 134–43.

16. Ibid., 140.

17. Rowan Williams, "The Sermon," in *Living the Eucharist: Affirming Catholicism Conference Papers*, eds. Steven Conway and David Stancliffe (London: Dartman, Longman, and Todd, 2001), 52.

18. Ibid., 45.

19. Ibid., 52–53. For Bonhoeffer on preaching as offering an apple, see Clyde E. Font, *Bonhoeffer: Worldly Preaching* (Nashville: Thomas Nelson, 1975), 112.

20. Williams, "The Sermon," 45.

21. John S. McClure, *Other-Wise Preaching: A Postmodern Ethic for Homiletics* (St. Louis: Chalice, 2001), 133–34.

22. John S. McClure, *The Roundtable Pulpit: Where Preaching and Leadership Meet* (Nashville: Abingdon, 1995).

23. Lose, *Confessing Jesus Christ*, 167. For key questions the confessional preacher asks of the biblical text, see 171 and 189–92.

24. For practical qualities in approaching a text and a sermon from the standpoint of otherness, see McClure, *Other-Wise Preaching*, 133–52.

Chapter 11 • Liberation Theologies and Preaching

1. On the social gospel, see Walter Rauschenbusch, *A Theology for the Social Gospel* (New York: Macmillan, 1917).

2. For an overview of issues in liberation theology today, see *The Cambridge Companion to Liberation Theology*, ed. Christopher Rowland, Cambridge Companions to Religion (Cambridge: Cambridge University Press, 1999).

3. For specific liberation theologies in North America, see *Handbook on U.S. Theologies of Liberation*, ed. Miguel A. De La Torre (St. Louis: Chalice, 2004).

4. Gayatri Spivak asks in a famous essay, "Can the Subaltern Speak?" in *Marxism and the Interpretation of Cultures*, ed. Cary Nelson and Lawrence Grossberg (Urbana: University of Illinois Press, 1988), 271–313.

5. Pablo Jiménez, "Toward a Postcolonial Homiletic: Justo L. González's Contribution to Hispanic Preaching," in *Hispanic Christian Thought at the Dawn of the Twenty-First Century: Apuntes in Honor of Justo L. González*, ed. Alvin Padilla, Robert Goizueta, Eldin Villafañe (Nashville: Abingdon, 2005), 167.

Chapter 12 • Ethnic Theologies and Preaching

1. Andrew Sung Park, *Racial Conflict and Healing: An Asian American Theological Perspective* (Maryknoll: Orbis, 1997), 103.

2. For example, Jung Young Lee, *Marginality: The Key to Multicultural Theology* (Minneapolis: Fortress Press, 1995).

3. Koo Yong Na, "Preaching and Cultural Context: A Case Study in Preaching in a Korean Context," in *Preaching in the Context of Worship*, ed. David M. Greenhaw and Ronald J. Allen (St. Louis: Chalice, 2000), 143.

4. Ibid., 141–45.

5. Jung Young Lee, *Korean Preaching: An Interpretation* (Nashville, Tenn.: Abingdon, 1997), 31.

6. Eunjoo Mary Kim, *Practicing the Presence of God: A Homiletic from an Asian American Perspective* (Valley Forge: Judson, 1999), 59–66.

7. Eunjoo Mary Kim, "A Korean American Perspective: Singing a New Song in a Strange Land," in *Justice Preaching: Ethnic and Cultural Perspectives*, ed. Christine Marie Smith (Cleveland: United Church Press, 1998), 103.

8. Henry H. Mitchell and Nicholas Cooper-Lewter, *Soul Theology: The Heart of American Black Culture* (Nashville: Abingdon, 1992), 37, 42, 59.

9. Henry H. Mitchell, *Black Preaching: The Recovery of a Powerful Art* (Nashville: Abingdon, 1990), 30–32, 56–59, 63–72, 78, 88–91, 92–93, 95–98.